THE
INCREDIBLE
EDIBLE
LANDSCAPE

Karen
Bastow

Joy
Bossi

THE INCREDIBLE EDIBLE LANDSCAPE

JOY BOSSI & KAREN BASTOW

HOBBLE CREEK PRESS

AN IMPRINT OF CEDAR FORT, INC.

SPRINGVILLE, UTAH

ISBN 13: 978-1-4621-1028-5

Published by CFI, an imprint of Cedar Fort, Inc., 2373 W. 700 S., Springville, UT 84663
Distributed by Cedar Fort, Inc., www.cedarfort.com

LIBRARY OF CONGRESS CATALOGING-IN-PUBLICATION DATA
Bossi, Joy, 1948-, author.
  The incredible edible landscape / Joy Bossi and Karen Bastow.
       p. cm.
  Includes index.
  ISBN 978-1-4621-1028-5
  1. Gardening. I. Bastow, Karen, 1953-, author. II. Title.

  SB450.97.B665 2011
  635--dc23

  2011043039

Cover and page design by Danie Romrell
Cover design © 2012 by Lyle Mortimer
Edited by Melissa J. Caldwell

Printed in China

10 9 8 7 6 5 4 3 2 1

Printed on acid-free paper

JOY'S DEDICATION

To my granddaughter: Gardeners love little birds—my new favorite is a tiny Wren. This book is a guide to loving a garden and the life-sustaining goodness that grows there. As she grows from a smiling little child to a young woman, I hope she remembers Grandma and knows Wren will always have Joy in her garden.

KAREN'S DEDICATION

To Steve, who gives me wings to soar yet keeps me firmly planted in rich soil. He sows seeds of courage and endurance, watered with patience and a gentle smile wherever he goes. Looking forward to walking through gardens of sunlight in eternity with you.

JOY'S ACKNOWLEDGMENTS

Over the years, loyal, kind listeners and viewers have greeted me and thanked me for helping them do well in their gardens. Some folks, who didn't even have gardens, still thanked me for brightening their days. Their encouragement brightened my days as well. The winding path that led me to become a gardening cheerleader took many, many turns. Who would have ever guessed this book was around the latest bend? Thank you for loving *Joy in the Garden*—and smile. I know you will always find joy in your garden! A hui hou!

KAREN'S ACKNOWLEDGMENTS

For all my friends and family (you know who you are) who have given so much love, support, and encouragement, along with helping hands and listening ears when it has been most needed. Couldn't do it without you!

AND TOGETHER, JOY AND KAREN ACKNOWLEDGE

Annette Boren, for keeping a couple of gardeners well-rooted. Thank you for your devoted friendship.

CONTENTS

INTRODUCTION:
Provident Gardening

> "The revelation to produce and store food may be as essential to our temporal welfare today as boarding the ark was to the people in the days of Noah." (Ezra Taft Benson, *Ensign*, Nov. 1980, 33.)

> "We encourage you to grow all the food that you feasibly can on your own property. . . . Grow vegetables and eat them from your own yard. Even those residing in apartments or condominiums can generally grow a little food in pots and planters. Study the best methods of providing your own foods. Make your garden . . . neat and attractive as well as productive. If there are children in your home, involve them in the process with assigned responsibilities." (Spencer W. Kimball, *Essentials of Home Production and Storage*, 2.)

Gardening is the all-time favorite hobby in America. Raised bed and beautiful row gardens abound. Almost everyone with even a postage stamp–size

WHAT IF THE SHELVES ARE EMPTY?

yard, a balcony, or a front step grows a few flowers or a potted tomato plant. Gardening is a great pastime, and those ripe, homegrown tomatoes are unsurpassed in taste. And when the frost signals the demise of that deliciousness, we heave a sigh of regret and begin to look forward to the next growing season. But what happens if we need to depend on what we grow for sustenance? What if our gardening turns from an "if it doesn't grow, I'll get it at the grocery store" mentality to a "this garden is vital because the stores are empty" necessity?

These what-ifs and a strong desire to heed the counsel of wise men and women have brought us, the authors, to share our ideas of gardening when it *really* counts. We call this *provident* gardening. The dictionary tells us that *provident* means "anticipating and making ready for future wants or emergencies; exercising foresight."[1] To us, provident gardening is to become more self-sufficient through growing our own food using traditional as well as non-traditional methods.

We each have our own perspective on provident gardening. Our ideas have been dovetailed into this book. As you read through an5d come to your own conclusions, we think it will help if you know some of our experiences. Here's Joy's take on the subject:

"In years gone way by, I worked in emergency preparedness, back when we still had Civil Defense Directors in every county. That designation changed to the Office of Comprehensive Emergency Management. FEMA, the Federal Emergency Management Administration, then took authority under the Department of Homeland Security.

"A committee I worked with wrote two booklets to be used in local schools. One, *I Can Make the Difference*, was targeted at the fourth-grade level, and high school students used the other, *Plan to Live*. The intent of both was to help students realize that no matter what the situation, their reactions and responses would be far more important than the actual cause of the emergency. Prepared for things that may happen, students would feel confident, empowered, and safer no matter what happened in their lives.

"I often thought, as I watched videos of people storming their local home improvement centers and grocery stores, that if folks would just take some simple precautions BEFORE there was a hurricane warning or flood warning or blizzard warning or tornado warning or initial jerk of an earthquake, how much better it would be for *everybody*.

"Those catastrophic occurrences certainly grab our attention and sometimes nearly shake our teeth loose. But the quiet happenings can also cause shrieks of alarm. E-coli here, Salmonella there . . . contaminants in our drinking water, loss of employment, isolation due to emergencies far from our local areas—things do happen. Now is the time to plan for what we can do to help ourselves and our families prepare for the difficulties that will surely come. We need to face these problems as adventures to be worked through together, not emergencies to be feared."

Karen, on the other hand, experienced the need for provident living in a more personal, day-to-day context:

"When the opportunity came to travel to Kenya and head up a humanitarian gardening project, I accepted with enthusiasm and, at the same time, trepidation. Along with a great team, I arrived at the Hands of Hope Safe House—basically a small

UNIMPROVED SITE

orphanage directed by Pastor Fred Afwai and his wife, Alice. Reality set in as my team and I surveyed the weed- and brush-covered garden site. At that moment, gardening took on a completely new meaning for me. My heart sank as I noted the dirty water that trickled through the lot, and I wondered if it contained raw sewage.

"Knowing that the twenty orphaned children who called the Safe House home were at times able to eat only every other day because of lack of food, transformed gardening as a hobby into gardening as a means of survival. It was imperative that we grew crops that flourished better than ever before. Fervent prayers by all were sent heavenward to bless this garden.

"Not wanting to introduce any equipment or supplies that would not be readily available in Kenya, we started with few tools. Several men and women traveled a long distance each day to learn, and they brought willing hands and happy hearts to the project.

Together we worked to clear brush, divert the stream of questionable water, and to construct 'boxes' made from rocks or blocks cemented together (so they wouldn't be stolen).

"We were able to plant some of the garden boxes, and I was amazed at how quickly the seeds germinated

and started to grow! It was heartwarming to see the people's reaction to knowing that food would soon be available. Six months later, it was even better to hear Pastor Fred say that the orphanage hadn't needed to buy vegetables since the first harvest. I was happy to know that hungry children were eating because of this garden project. They have continued to expand these gardens and fill the area with garden boxes, as well as add other enterprises such as the raising of cows and chickens, a mushroom-growing operation, and even a bio-fuel system for cooking.

"This humbling experience taught me the need to learn and practice the skills of provident gardening for our own times of need. I gained a deeper appreciation for the abundance we so often enjoy."

Some people feel confident that their storage covers all the basic needs and maybe even some extras for emotional comfort. Perhaps you or your family has been working slowly and consistently at filling your preparedness supplies. But there is nothing like putting your storage to the test by staging a mock disaster of your own. Name the crisis whatever you want: earthquake, flood, winter storm (it's more comfortable to practice this one in the spring/summer/fall months),

trucker strike, tornado, or hurricane. Of course water and many other essentials are needed, but in this book, we take a look at future needs as seen from a gardener's perspective.

Have you ever tried living on what you have in your home for one week without sneaking out to the store for Chips Ahoy and milk? Could you reach into your storage for vegetables and fruit? Do you have bottled peaches, dried tomatoes, or frozen strawberries? Could you step into your garden for lettuce, spinach, or fresh tomatoes? Do you know how to start little veggie plants from seed? Do you *have* any veggie seeds? Is fertilizer listed on your go-buy-it-soon list?

For those who have gardened before, was your first garden a blooming success? Could you have eaten long from your bountiful harvest that first time around? If you haven't taken the challenge of growing simple, unassuming little carrots, you may be unpleasantly surprised. Growing carrots from seed is a tricky procedure unless you learn the correct techniques. Even practiced carrot growers find some years are better than others, and some gardens won't even push up a single orange gem. How do you find out if you can even grow carrots?

Only by trying in your own spot or pot of soil will you know what edibles you can grow. And success one year doesn't necessarily indicate a great harvest the next season. Variables can throw even experienced gardeners for a loop. Frost, flood, hail, howling wind, drought, late frost, weeds, hungry insects, hungry birds, romping dogs, digging cats, weeds, early frost, late snow, soil diseases, and vacations can result in the best planned and planted garden producing abso-bloominlutely nothing.

Being provident isn't just about the form, design, or size of a garden; it's about using space to produce food and add beauty to your surroundings. Your emotional, mental, and spiritual well-being is as important as feeding the physical self. At any given time it may be more important to be able to smile at the little face of a Johnny Jump Up than it is to make soup out of your own homegrown vegetables.

Sitting with loved ones in the shade of the walnut tree and recalling some of Grandma's stories may have much more influence on their lives than the nutrition found in the harvested walnuts. Fruit and nut trees make just as much shade as a comparable sized ornamental tree. And the large, productive apricot tree climbs just as easily as a maple tree. Children run along paths bordered by herbs and flowers just as merrily as little paths running through only petunias and geraniums. A brush by a mint patch or lemon verbena plant will make for super memories of something enticing and associated with Grandma.

An edible landscape is one step toward creating a provident garden. In the beginning, there was a garden, and the garden was good.

> God almighty first planted a garden. And, indeed, it is the purest of human pleasures.
> —Sir Francis Bacon

But it takes a diligent gardener to keep it good. Knowing where seeds come from, how to get little plants started from those seeds, and how to get seeds back from those plants puts you a little nearer to a provident garden. Another step is learning how to

prepare the produce from the garden. Preparing delicious veggies gives a sense of accomplishment to the gardener and cook, whether or not they are one and the same person.

Sharing your bounty slides you even further along the gardening spectrum in your quest to become a provident gardener. You may share with the daughter and son-in-law who live across town. Maybe the recipient will be the older gardener across the street who just can't garden the way they used to. Perhaps you'll take bags of produce to the nearest food pantry. There may be still more coming from the garden than you can give away or eat while it is at its freshest. Freeze, dry, or bottle the surplus, and you have become a frugal, forethoughtful provident gardener.

Come walk with us down the garden path. We invite and encourage you to garden more providently in your own yard and garden. Start small—put into practice one new skill at a time and soon you will be ready to claim your title of Provident Gardener.

Thyme to Dig In

Whenever you see this symbol throughout the book, know it's "Thyme to Dig In" to discover a useful hint or tip!

NOTE

1. Standard Dictionary, as found in *Recent Statutes*, Fordham Law Review, vol. 10, 443 (1941), http://ir.lawnet.fordham.edu/flr/vol10/iss3/5.

Chapter 1: If the Edible Fits, Plant It!

Everyone has a vision of the perfect garden and yard. From what they would like to grow to what kind of trees and bushes to plant, both young and seasoned gardeners have a plan of some sort. And they learn something new every season. Although trial and error can teach new ideas, a less painful way to learn is from those gardeners who have already tried other methods.

We can learn from books, neighbors, or history. One such resource is Thomas Jefferson (yes, that Thomas Jefferson), who ran an amazing garden at Monticello and lived for the chance to add a new plant to his repertoire. By necessity, he invented and developed new methods and approaches to fruit and vegetable gardening. If he hadn't made such an impressive reputation as politician and president, he would surely have been hailed by the entire world as the premier horticulturist of his time.

> Though an old man, I am but a young gardener.
> —Thomas Jefferson

It would be hard to duplicate the gardens at Monticello, but with a little research, you can discover Mr. Jefferson's favorite plants. You may want to try each one of them. But you may also talk to other gardeners and be influenced to specialize in only tomatoes.

Some gardeners become "collectors" and seek out every new variety of a specific plant. Others have never met a plant they didn't love! They think, "Surely there is a place somewhere in my garden for this!" You may slide between the two extremes depending on what you find growing in a friend's garden or what is on sale at the local nursery. At times you may jump at the chance to grow something you love to eat, like blueberries or avocados. Even though you are told that those plants just won't do well where you live, you try anyway. Don't ever let a little failure like a dead blueberry plant or an avocado seed that won't grow discourage you from trying to grow something you love.

EDIBLE LANDSCAPE

What is an edible landscape? It is placing edible or fruit-producing plants in unconventional places and in unconventional ways in the yard—often right in the existing landscape. To undertake provident gardening means to *try, try, try* to grow something that will enrich your future. Something to eat is surely part of this kind of garden. We know vegetables play well with ornamental flowers and shrubs, so an integrated planting can fill the need for "pretty" and still be "edible."

COLORFUL CABBAGE IN A FLOWER BED

There is no reason harvest and beauty can't go hand in hand. Inspect your current landscape for an area that will do just that. A couple of red cabbage plants will absolutely shine as they begin to mature among the zinnias. Chives poking up through white alyssum create a crisp combination in a little pot. An artichoke plant, while only an annual where we live, makes an incredible focal point in a mostly ornamental garden. And when it's time to harvest, leaving one of those artichokes on the plant will present a unique purple, fuzzy flower to amaze you and your neighbors.

Some provident gardeners have very little space or prefer even more of an integrated gardenscape. They tuck their herbs in the flower garden, use berry bushes for a hedge, cover a fence with grape vines perhaps to screen an undesirable view, plant nut and fruit trees in the park strip, brighten the flowerbed with colorful Swiss chard, let the winter squash ramble above the ground through the scrub oak, use carrots as a border in the annual flower garden, grow ten different vegetables in containers around the patio, and pot up some basil to use in the kitchen.

So now let's take a look at some additional ways to increase the production of your little acre, half acre, $\frac{1}{50}$ of an acre, or three pots on the windowsill.

Thyme to Dig In

But you look around and don't see *any* room for a garden in your present location. Do you have a pot of geraniums? Tuck in a small hot pepper plant! Do you have large containers with dracaena, petunias, and Bacopa? Plant zucchini, carrots, and basil instead. Leave a little lawn for your pooch and plant tomatoes in the rest using a raised bed or box garden. Try nut trees in the front yard to take the place of flowering ornamental fruit trees. Oh yes, there are ways!

Thyme to Dig In

An edible landscape can even provide places to play. Children, grandchildren, nieces or nephews, or the neighbor kids just love to play in a large teepee completely surrounded and overgrown with pole beans. Kids will love hiding in it but will be completely oblivious to the fact that those beans will be used during the winter for their favorite green bean casserole. Let whimsy be a part of your garden and your life.

THE BEGINNING

When you take a good look around your existing landscape, do you see any plants that are currently or will eventually produce something you could eat? Is there a dedicated space for a vegetable garden? Any fruit trees? Berry bushes? A separate herb garden? Grape vines? If you eat the produce you are growing, put up or store the harvest, and share with others what you and your family have in excess, you are well on your way to becoming a provident gardener.

If, however, few of those items are found in your garden, it's time to make some changes. Ask yourself some questions such as, "What do I like to eat?" But don't ask, "What do I want to *grow?*" or you may be sorry. Even if radishes and onions are near foolproof, it won't make you happy when your family has a bountiful harvest and THEN you remember that only one member of the family even *likes* radishes and that onions aren't *anybody's* favorite. Choose the veggies you most like to eat first, and then try one or two new ones each year. You may discover a real love for homegrown brussels sprouts and be surprised that it is also an unusual and attractive plant to feature in the landscape.

Thyme to Dig In	Brush up on the pollination requirements for fruiting plants. For instance, Bartlett pears will produce with only one tree planted, but a second tree will boost the harvest. Apple varieties can be very finicky about what pollen will be accepted to produce fruit. And very few sweet cherries are self-fertile; most need a second kind of cherry to pollinate the flowers.

There will always be a call for the stand-apart vegetable garden, but when space is a major factor in the growing process, integration will be a great help. Herbs too are often thought of as only growing in an official, organized "herb garden." Try to visualize the beauty of a border of purple ruffle basil, a tasty ground cover of golden creeping thyme, or a sparkling addition of tricolor sage in the front planting beds.

CONTAINERS

Most anything you'd like to eat can be grown in a container. Well, maybe not pizza directly, but you can plant a few containers, each with a tomato, pepper, oregano, basil, or onions. You're on your own for the crust, but, hey, a poor little garden container can only do so much!

Little plants, like beets and spinach, can be grown in small containers; however, peppers and tomatoes should be in pots at least 14 inches wide and deep. Even little shallow pots can grow lettuce, green onions, and radishes. It will take something at least the size of a half whiskey barrel to grow the larger produce like winter squash or melons.

A group of different-sized containers is very appealing to the eye and can support a variety of crops. Nearly anything that can hold soil and has some drainage can be used as unconventional containers—washtubs, buckets, wooden crates, old shoes and boots, even plastic grocery bags in a pinch—the list is endless.

Containers need good drainage holes—holes that are large enough so the soil doesn't clog them but also allow for good drainage. If the hole is too large, soil will leak out the bottom. A large rock placed loosely over the hole, an old nylon stocking, or even a folded piece of newspaper can prevent soil loss while still allowing excess water to drain.

Resist the temptation to fill a container with yard dirt or you'll end up attempting to grow plants in a weed-filled near-cement environment. You get what you pay for when filling the container with potting soil, so wisely choose a good mix full of all the nutrients needed for healthy plant growth. Make sure the soil has been moistened thoroughly before planting.

Crops in containers dry out quickly and need frequent watering. Since vegetables are over 95 percent water, allowing them to dry out even temporarily can reduce the yield. No matter the watering method you choose, *water*, *water*, *water* regularly.

Growing in containers has some nice advantages. One is the matter of keeping ahead of the weeds. Competition for water and nutrients put most weeds very high on the gardener's hit list. The very fact that we call those plants weeds tells us that they are supremely adept at rapid root growth and sucking the water out of all the nearby soil. Their ability to multiply puts bunnies to shame. However, the only weeds you will find in your container either blew in or were dropped in by a passing bird. Pulling these teeny weeds from a six-inch pot beats wrestling existing wild morning glory two out of three falls (or autumns) and losing every time.

Containers can be mobile, and that is another advantage. Put wheels under heavy pots or just pick up the little ones. You can move cool weather crops, like lettuce, to the shade. This will prolong the harvest before the plant bolts to seed. (Chapter 3 will explain bolting.) Sun-loving crops need 6–8 hours of direct sun daily, so move these plants to the sunniest locations.

Thyme to Dig In

Self-watering containers are a great idea to ensure proper watering—especially when the gardener is on vacation. Expensive versions are readily available, but consider the homemade version developed by Wayne Burleson from Montana. Wayne's inexpensive and provident portable bucket gardens work great. Leaving the handle attached makes it easy to transport the garden to the safety of the garage when frost threatens. Check it out at www.pasturemanagement.com/Howtobucketgarden.htm.

INDOOR GARDENING

Why not try to have a container with edibles indoors? With the right amount of light, this is certainly possible. However, sticking with the leafy greens usually works best (that's lettuce, spinach, chard, and radishes).

Why, you could even plant a variety of colorful lettuce with chives spiking in the center, use it as a table centerpiece, and then harvest as you eat! Also, if you're lucky enough to have a greenhouse—use it! You can find scads of information about growing all kinds of plants indoors from your local county extension office.

RAISED BEDS

Out of all the gardening methods, raised beds are Karen's personal favorite (with edible landscaping rapidly advancing to second place). Though reluctant at first to give up a more traditional single-row garden, Karen and her family decided to convert one-half of their garden area to raised beds. It didn't take long to realize that the single-row portion was a lot more work and required more weeding. By the next season, the entire garden was converted to raised beds!

How do we love thee? Let us count the ways that raised beds encourage and delight gardeners:

1. Anything growing outside of the designated beds can be declared a weed and dispatched forthwith. Or you can use lawn grass for the paths and just mow the "weeds" down. Add a commercial weed barrier, cardboard, or a thick layer of newspaper under the soil inside the beds to prevent weed growth from coming up from existing soil.

2. Pests like gophers can be kept at bay by lining the bottom of the "box" with something like hardware cloth.

3. Water can be directed to just the plants you want and not the undesirable plants in the paths between beds.

4. Soil raised above ground level warms more quickly in the spring.

5. Raised soil also drains effectively.

6. With the correct height of border material, gardeners can sit to do the chores in the garden; or those who cannot get down (or up) can do their gardening at chair or standing height.

7. Because of a more compact size, raised

beds are more easily protected from late spring or early fall frosts.

8. Insects and birds can be blocked from their usual mayhem. Just cover the boxes with something like floating row cover.

9. The garden is easily kept tidy, and a tidy garden makes for an enticing garden.

Creating beds bordered by cinderblocks, rocks, wood, plastic, or vinyl fencing clearly defines the planting area. But you can also use free-form raised beds—soil that is raised in height from the paths around it and has gently sloping sides. These are one of the easiest and least expensive ways to start raised-bed gardening. Just lower the paths and pile that excess soil onto the beds as illustrated.

It's hard to think of any disadvantages of raised beds. After much cogitating, only two come to mind: wood boxes eventually rot and need to be replaced, and a raised bed may dry out quicker and need more watering. (But then, less water overall is used because

of the smaller area watered.) Not much of a discouraging word here!

Both styles of raised beds have a fantastic added advantage: you can amend the soil without wasting good compost in areas that won't be growing plants. It is easier to maintain and contain soil in the beds with solid sides, especially if you are growing in a "soil-less" mix. That mix could be straight potting soil, a blend of your own design, or a bagged product formulated especially for use in raised bed growing. Whatever is used, it is imperative that the mix contains a good variety of different types of organic matter.

Joy used the formless method for years by tilling in different directions and forming new beds for each growing season. She never created a hardpan layer from running the tiller over and over the soil in the same direction every year. The sloping sides seemed to stay put just fine. (The real reason for this ever-changing pattern of the beds was probably that she couldn't decide on what look she wanted permanently for her back garden.)

The permanent design came later when the available growing space declined. Some very large trees had started shading too much of the garden area, and the time had come to make every inch as productive as possible. Plus, Joy sold her tiller and started a do-it-herself project. And the project needed to stay within a meager budget.

Because Joy didn't have secondhand material like used boards, chunks of concrete, or discarded plastic, she settled on redwood. Then she was off to the lumber department to choose size and length. But before making those decisions, she stopped right in the middle of the redwood aisle and inhaled deeply. She loved the smell of freshly cut wood! For her beds, which were 4, 8, and 12 feet long, she decided on 2 x 10-inch redwood. That was a considerable amount of lumber. The beds were either 2 or 4 feet wide, so her pocketbook dictated the decision of how many beds to start building.

Joy had previously amended the garden soil in that area and excavated the enormous number of rocks that had been there (see *Joy in Your Garden*, page 4, for an explanation of the rocks). She used the existing soil in addition to four bags of excellent compost per 4 square feet to fill the boxes. Since weeding is nearly nonexistent and watering is just in the boxes, gardening time is minimal. That is to say, garden *maintenance* time is minimal. Her enjoyment time is way up!

SINGLE ROW GARDENS

Provident gardens can be found in the long-standing tradition of single-row growing. In fact, that was the form that the original American provident garden

always took. Ground was broken by hand or plow, seeds planted by hand, and crops watered by seasonal rain, hand-carried buckets, or flood and row irrigation. These are the gardens your great-grandfather or great-grandmother counted on to feed the family. Good years meant an abundance of gleaming jars in the pantry, squash waiting on the shelves, and apples and potatoes down in the cellar.

More likely a garden in this day and age is something on a much smaller scale. We know of a couple that had absolutely no growing space in the back of the house. A desire for fresh vegetables drove them to try, a little timidly at first, a plot of veggies next to the driveway out front. Out went the lawn. Neighbors looked from windows with eyebrows a little raised. Then in went a lovely border of lavender. Ah, a flower garden, the folks along the street were thinking. But no, because then the couple installed a drip system to water little 4-foot rows of beets and carrots!

Neighbors now came out to casually walk down the street and couldn't help but stop to inquire about the new garden. Before the couple knew it, their little row garden had become the neighborhood gathering place! Eggplants with their lovely flowers and amethyst fruit joined a couple of pepper plants and, of course, three tomato plants. Plenty of produce was shared among the neighbors who stopped by, and the next year, little front gardens were popping up in other yards.

A provident garden needn't be something different from what you are used to. You can choose a little more variety of vegetables. Or dedicate an entire section or row to just one crop; that way you will harvest enough to store as well as eat fresh. Memories will be stirred when you open a gleaming quart of peaches. When you went to Grandma's house (you tell your kids), you would make a whole meal out of bottled peaches from grandpa's tree and grandma's homemade bread.

The garden again becomes a place of teaching provident principles when you explain why you are growing extra peppers or squash. Food banks are always short of fresh produce, so one or more rows are set aside for sharing. You could make it a family project to grow, harvest, and share the dedicated vegetables or fruit. For example, "Fresh from the Heart" is a program in Salt Lake City, Utah, that encourages all homeowners to grow a little more produce than the family needs. Then they can take the extra to an organization that distributes to those who have no access to a garden. Start a similar program in your neighborhood or town. It is a grow-share-win idea!

WATER

Even in cities and suburbs, some fortunate gardeners enjoy using secondary water. Secondary water is not culinary quality water. It is sometimes supplied by canal or delivered through a pressurized system, making watering quite easy and inexpensive. Use secondary water for the garden, but don't drink it.

Water rights have caused many a quarrel, even fights, in the arid west. It is still possible to find land worth a good deal less than the water shares that go with it. Secondary water supplied to a garden may be less expensive than culinary water, but it may carry other costs that a gardener needs to consider. Water turns may come in the middle of the night and won't come again for maybe ten days. Weed seeds are carried from upstream right to your garden. And if you happen to be near the end of the canal supply, salts from runoff into the canal can occasionally build up to a level that can damage crops.

It is far more likely in these days that a gardener will be using culinary water on their garden. Water is a finite commodity. Land development leads to more and more people using the same finite supply, creating a dilemma. There just isn't enough to go around. Water to drink versus water for the garden—gardens lose every time. Conservation is the cry; water-wise the slogan.

Row irrigation water loses some water due to evaporation, as does flood irrigation. When the choice is possible, use drip or soaker systems; they help conserve water.

DRIP SYSTEM

Determine the needs of your crops, the type of soil in your garden, and how much your system delivers. Even if you are hauling a watering can out to the garden for only one pumpkin or to the two potted tomatoes on the deck, be sure the soil actually needs more water before adding more. The water meter at the end of your wrist is an excellent tool. Stick your

finger down 3 or 4 inches into the soil. Moisture indicates that you can wait another day to water.

Sandy soil will not hold moisture well, and the plants growing in it will need more frequent applications of water. Clay soil holds moisture, but water soaks in so slowly that much will just run off if you try to dump water on the garden. Slow application or several passes with the water will be more likely to make it down to the thirsty roots.

If you are blessed with land and sufficient water, the row garden can be exceptionally productive. And the produce is usually sufficient to begin the stocking up process. If you only have a little row of carrots bordering your front garden, it isn't likely you will be drying many for winter use. But if you have two 20-foot rows of carrots . . . well, there you go! It's time for the dehydrator to come up from the basement or the pressure canner to get its yearly pressure check.

INTENSIVE AND SUCCESSION PLANTING

In an already-established vegetable garden, your harvest can be increased by intensive planting—planting crops closer together in blocks. Did you ever wonder why planting guidelines for carrots indicate they need to be spaced 3 inches apart on each side but must have 12 to 15 inches beween rows? How would carrots know to only spread out in two of the four directions? The spacing often suggested in some gardening books and most seed packets assume you need 12 or 24 or 36 inches to get your plow between the rows! All that room isn't needed in most gardens now, so cozy up those plants right next to each other to make better use of the space in the garden.

A proven way to harvest more from your garden is to plant again, in the same place, as soon as harvesting an early crop opens up space in the garden. Succession planting is just that—a method of using the same little piece of garden area to grow two or even three crops in one season. Beans and summer squash can replace the early lettuce and peas. Just add good compost to that spot of soil and plant the second crop. If you plant bush beans so the entire harvest comes on pretty much at the same time, in can go a second planting of spinach and chard. Sometimes this works very well, but "even though a gardener proposes, weather often disposes." Just plan on providing the plants some extra protection against an early frost. If this late season attempt doesn't give you much to show for your effort, you can always hope for better luck next year.

INCREASING GARDEN SPACE

A gentle transition can be made to a provident garden. Someone in the family is probably going to raise a bit of a ruckus if you suggest digging up all the lawn and plant a small orchard in the backyard or if you propose to plow under the front flower garden and plant tomatoes and peppers instead. We suggest, however, that in small increments, some lawn can be reduced and an integrated garden begun. This will reduce the missing-the-lawn shock considerably. There may be restrictive covenants or HOA regulations to consider, but you can check on that before beginning.

BRIDAL WREATH AND SQUASH VINES

SWISS CHARD AND PANSIES

CABBAGE IN FLOWER BED

Start by planting, for instance, Purple basil with the marigolds in the front garden. Then, when it is time to replace the Blue Spruce that blew over in a horrendous windstorm, plant a group of three to five hazelnut trees, creating a little grove in that same space.

In the only corner exposed to full sun that is now backyard lawn, cut a diagonal strip, creating a triangle of grass that can be taken out or plowed under. Next, put a little white picket fence along that newly cut edge of lawn with a little opening in the middle, and—voila—a wonderful little nook for growing, say, tomatoes and peppers and rutabagas.

Do you have trouble with that lawn along the sidewalk that always needs extra water? You know the place—always full of weeds and ants. Because concrete and turf do not peacefully coexist, you can eliminate many problems by just removing the lawn! Not all of the lawn, just a three-foot swath along the cement. That border can now be planted with herbs.

Perhaps you would like a formal little hedge. Lavender trims neatly to make a lovely evergreen (ever "gray-green" actually) border. Lemon thyme could be dotted along the way for a more informal look. If you choose Opal basil, you can add a dash of surprising color. Eggplant has very attractive flowers and could be used as a sort of bookend arrangement: have an eggplant on each end and the herbs in the middle. Carrot foliage is a fluffy, annual fern-look-alike. Combined with Bright Lights Chard, the two create an eye-catching color combination. Early in the spring, those borders could be festooned with a dozen different colors of lettuce planted willy-nilly or laid out in a quilt-like pattern.

Whew! And those are just the first little bits of provident replacements in the gardens. Gradually the garden areas become more productive, and the lawn area shrinks. Now, lest you think we have no use for turf grass, we think you should keep the lawn that is doing what lawn does best: it gives kids a place to play, contributes a lovely green accent to the landscape, cools the surrounding areas, and keeps the mud covered up. Realize, however, that lawn is usually growing in the space that receives the most hours of sunshine in your yard. That is prime edible growing area. If the only thing your grass is doing is giving someone an excuse to use a riding lawnmower or maybe making money for the local purveyor of weed killer and fertilizer, then replacement may not be such an untenable idea.

TREES IN THE LANDSCAPE

Old standard apple and cherry trees grow to be 25–30 (or more) feet tall. Grown as shade trees with incidental fruit, they need very little care and very little water. Since they also grow to be 25–30 feet wide, space is gobbled up quickly with not much that can be grown underneath them, except maybe a little lawn. For home production, there are far better choices than full standard fruit trees.

Semi-dwarf fruit trees start slowing down at about half the size of a standard tree. With consistent pruning most of these trees can be kept in the 8–12

DWARF NAGAMI KUMQUAT TREE

foot range. A semi-dwarf peach tree produces at least 1–2 bushels of fruit, and that supplies a nice home production of bottled peaches, peach jam, and peach leather. Peach trees make a fine little mini-orchard when three or four are planted grouped together. Leave about 8 feet between trunks, and you can prune to keep them in their own space.

Dropping down a size, the choice of true dwarf trees is a tad more limited in the different varieties sold. But having a tree that can be kept under 6 feet tall where you can pick ripe fruit just by walking a few feet from your front or back door is amazing. It puts a fresh fruit supply within the realm of possibility for those with even very small garden or lawn spaces.

DWARF FRUIT TREE GARDEN

At the bottom of the size range are the mini fruit trees. Little mini trees were developed to be grown in containers, and their heights range from 3 to 4 feet tall. As long as you can give them enough sun, they will show their gratitude by displaying lovely spring blossoms followed by several tasty fruits.

Regardless of the size of the tree, for the fruit to form (after the showy blossoms do their come-hither to pollinating insects), the pollen must be compatible with the little interior parts of the flowers. If the pollen from the same variety of fruit tree is compatible, the variety is said to be self-fertile. Upshot of that is you will get production even if you plant only one tree of each variety. Most peaches, nectarines, and apricots are self-fertile—except for the J. H. Hale peach. Most apples and cherries are *not* self-fertile and will need another variety to pollinate and produce fruit. Pears, especially Bartlett, are partially self-fertile, so you will get some fruit from a single tree but the yield is greatly increased if another Bartlett pear is growing somewhere within a couple of blocks of your tree.

Dwarf fruit trees lend themselves to being nestled in an existing landscape. You can create a hedge, grove, ornamental focal point, or just a cute row of little trees. Even the dreaded park strip becomes productive when you plant small nut and fruit trees in this problem-prone space. Since the trees need only infrequent watering once established, there is no need for a full-on sprinkling system. If the system is already in place, trade out the spray heads for smaller drip emitters. It works best if the area is on a separate valve so the timing can be different than the lawn and other thirstier garden areas.

One of the real advantages of growing the smaller-sized trees is quite noticeable when it is time to prune every spring. Yep, *every* spring. No more balancing on a ladder or climbing to reach a top branch.

Safety and ease encourages keeping up with a yearly schedule. Skipping a year, or more, drastically reduces the quality of the fruit and the health of the tree. Remember why you chose the semi- or true dwarf tree in the first place: luscious fruit. Now that should keep you motivated enough to be diligent.

> Gardens are not made by singing "Oh, how beautiful," and sitting in the shade.
> —Rudyard Kipling

Pruning, thinning the fruit, and insect control make for the greatest production of fruit. All of these duties are much easier when you deal with a small tree, but each of the projects are still work (see *Joy in Your Garden*, 93). This is a small and relatively pleasant price to pay for homegrown produce. And should you have only a tiny harvest from your smallish trees, you can still preserve the goodness by making fruit leather. It doesn't take a bushel or two for this process. Freezer jam can also be made in batches using only a small amount of fresh fruit or a few green tomatoes. Yes, green tomatoes make a remarkable jam that tastes just like fresh raspberry jam.

Mock Raspberry Jam
(from Margie Wemsley)

5 cups green tomatoes, ground or blended
5 cups sugar
Boil, stirring until sugar is dissolved.
Add 1 6-oz. package raspberry Jell-O
Cook for 25 minutes, stirring often.
Pour into jars, process in boiling bath for 15 minutes
Makes 9½ pint jars.

OTHER PLANTS THAT KEEP ON GIVING

Some productive little plants take up even less space than small trees. Some can be grown in pots or tucked in existing landscapes. You can change the entire feel of a garden with just a few additions. For instance, are you spending more time in your own little corner of the world? Do you want to make it look like a tropical paradise? Rhubarb growing in a sunny place with plenty of water looks like a South Seas island: leaves that are 2–3 feet across, pink to green stems, and a zany flower stalk that comes right up through the middle! Cozy that up against a 4 x 4-foot block of bamboo (aka corn), plunk down a couple of Canna lilies with the striped leaves and fluorescent flowers, and we tell ya, it's a tropical paradise just waiting for a little drink with an umbrella.

YELLOW FLOOFY STEMS

Asparagus is one of the few perennial vegetables we have that does well in zones 4 and 5. Rather than planting it way out back (if you have a way out back), try letting it be a lovely screen along one of your property lines closer to the house. Maybe even on both sides of the gate leading from the front to the backyard. A well-prepared bed can supply asparagus for years and years. Then comes the bonus—in the fall, the wispy stems called "fern" become a blaze of yellow, floofy, feathery stems. Gorgeous.

The best-known edibles that live for years and years are bushes, canes, and vines. The cane types include raspberries, blackberries, and all their cousins, plus currant, quince, fig, gooseberry, and blueberry bushes.

BLACKBERRIES

Anywhere a flowering shrub grows and has enough sun to bloom regularly can be a place for another incredible edible.

For example, a recent winter went through the Wasatch Front gardens like death wielding a scythe. Roses died by the hundreds. Now, we're not wishing harm to any of your rose bushes, but let's imagine you had a lovely rose hedge along one side of your property. No fence, just the hedge. Blessings on the thorn bushes that happened to have roses, they prevented anybody from cutting through that part of the garden. But what if something happened and the rose hedge died? Instead of planting more roses, you have other alternatives to consider.

Two of the thorniest plants we know are the blackberry and the gooseberry. The blackberry has recurved thorns, meaning you can push your hand in, but be ready for a transfusion when you try to pull your hand back out. That only happens when you or somebody trying to cut through your yard doesn't take a properly slow approach to the blackberry thicket. Gooseberry bushes, on the other hand, have just straightforward, 1-inch long, super strong spines all along every branch.

GOOSEBERRIES

GRAPE VINES ON A TRELLIS

Of course, of the two, blackberries and the related boysenberries, loganberries, dewberries, and so on, are by far the tastier of the two thorny protectors. Seems like, however, every child over the age of six ought to have the indelible memory of some loving adult handing them a very large gooseberry and saying, "Sure, you can eat it. Go ahead." If you feel your jaws tightening and your tongue curling up even as you read that last sentence, we'll bet it is a memory of a gooseberry crashing out from your past.

Planting white, red, golden, or black currants would make a gentler, kinder, thornless hedge. Golden currant is a Utah native that has flowers that smell of cloves and berries that, if the birds will leave you some, are quite tasty. Red currants need to be planted in groups only because you will want a heavy harvest to make currant jelly. Superb! And the only way it can possibly be improved upon is by adding a few raspberries to the pot. In an area with quite acid soil, blueberries can be used as a hedge as well. Should you happen to have alkaline soil, as most gardeners in the Intermountain West do, blueberries will struggle and look pathetic until you have pity and dig them up. Perhaps it isn't quite that bad, but it is close. Blueberries thrive in soil with a pH of around 4.5. But in this area, soil is often in the range of 7.5 to 7.8. Gardeners are accustomed to adding tons of organic matter, figuratively and sometimes literally speaking, just to bring the pH down to near neutral 7. To compensate for this huge difference, you will need to grow in nearly straight peat moss, using an acidifying fertilizer. Be aware that even your water may be alkaline. It is getting easier to find local stores carrying blueberry plants, enticing you with the luscious pictures on the containers. We have two words for you: Good luck.

Grapevines live for decades and produce in spite of many a gardener's neglect. Actually a little benign neglect can cover a great lack of knowledge or time. To get the greatest production, pruning should be done diligently every year and can be taken to an art form. We recommend you get a good book, like *The Pruning Book* by Lee Reich, or take a class from your local county extension office. Should you only want to cover the fence to block an unsightly view or grow the fruit for grape juice, jelly, or raisins, here are a few things to keep in mind:

- Grapevines can put on 15–20 feet of growth per year. A chain-link fence will restrict the pruning to just the vines that are sticking out perpendicular to the fence.

- Grapes (the fruit) grow on the current year's new growth—no fruit grows on any of the vines left from previous years. After the fifth year, it is nearly impossible to prune too much.

- In cold winter areas, grapes pruned later than February or very early March will look like they are bleeding to death. They aren't. The clear sap will slow down and eventually stop, at least by the time the leaves start to show up.

- Grapevines do climb using little twisty tendrils. Any nearby tree looks identical to a trellis as far as a grapevine can tell.

Edible perennials create a bonus harvest for years to come and enhance your landscape as well! Trees, shrubs, and cane fruit can be tailored to your individual garden, whatever shape or size it may be. We invite you to use the ideas in this chapter as kindling to light the fire that will warm through the years as you grow and enjoy your harvest.

Chapter 2: Have Your Garden and Eat It Too

Work is part of the natural investment made by those who aim to be provident gardeners. Work is strength of mind over inertia—once in motion, a gardener can see more clearly, think more positively, and breathe more deeply. Gardening isn't all work, but without the effort, gardening becomes a drudge. That's right. *Without* the effort, gardeners just putter around wondering what happened to their dream of a gorgeous, productive landscape.

An edible landscape is rarely carefree—unless the container full of leafy basil and the large pot with a single tomato, both placed near the edge of the patio, *is* your edible landscape, in which case perhaps *carefree* is a comfortable description. Once your "garden" expands to include multiple containers, raised beds, integrated planting areas, or irrigated rows, *carefree* will disappear from your gardening vocabulary.

CHOCOLATE CHIP COOKIE BUSH

That said, there is no reason fun and whimsy can't be part of the gardening work as well. Years ago Joy's good friend was preparing a garden with the help of her little grandson. Together they planted peas, carrots, beans, tomatoes, and lettuce. Straightening up with a little sigh, Nate said, "Grandma, couldn't we plant some cookies too?" When Joy heard this story, she decided that was just what her friend's garden needed—a Chocolate Chip Cookie Bush! When Joy explained what she wanted to do, her friend laughed and said, "Sure! Go for it!" The little boy's uncle overheard the conversation and later said, "While you're at it, have Joy plant a beef jerky bush for me."

Nate's third birthday arrived, and the family invited Joy to the party. The night before, she made small chocolate chip cookies using mini-chocolate chips. While the cookies were hot out of the oven, Joy used a plastic drinking straw to punch a small hole in each one. And so Nate's uncle wouldn't feel left out, Joy also bought several pieces of beef jerky and, using a hole punch, poked a hole in the end of each piece. Early on the day of the party, she took the little cookies and jerky to Nate's grandma's backyard. There was a nice sized lilac bush near the corner of the house. Joy carefully cut a few leaves off but left the petioles on the branches. From each leaf stem she hung a little cookie, keeping them down low so little Nate could reach them. Using the same technique as the lilac leaves, Joy hung the jerky from a Red Twig Dogwood growing near the fence.

When it was time for the party, the little birthday boy came out with the basket his grandma had given him to "harvest" his present. His eyes grew big, and a smile to match lit up his face. "Oh, Grandma, you did plant cookies!" The little basket was soon filled with the fruit of the cookie bush. Joy nudged Nate's uncle and said, "There's a bush back there you might like too." As he turned toward the fence, laughter broke out from everyone, because the fruit of the jerky bush was ripe and ready for picking!

Going a step further, Joy decided there ought to be a botanically and technically correct paper written to explain the phenomenon of the Chocolate Chip Cookie Bush, so she wrote "Biscuitus Deliciosa." (See appendix for complete "scientific" paper.)

Choosing what to grow in the provident garden is limited only by imagination. Once you open your mind to a possible Chocolate Chip Cookie Bush, your imagination can take you where no garden has gone before. Come explore with us various types of gardens that will produce the makings for some all-time favorites. For instance, how about a garden dedicated to all things vegetable that can be put into green Jell-O!

Biscuitus Deliciosa

If you haven't grown your own from seed, you have missed one of the greatest garden treats around for the novice gardener. Seeds need an incubation time of 10 minutes in a 350-degree oven. For the best germination and development, a growth medium of the following nutrients is recommended:

2¾ cups flour

I tsp. baking powder

I tsp. baking soda

I tsp. salt

Thoroughly sift these powders together.

Cream very well the following nutrients:

I cup butter

¾ cup white sugar

¾ cup brown sugar

2 tsp. vanilla

When light and fluffy, add 2 eggs, mixing well after each egg.

Add the dry ingredients gradually and mix well.

When this seedbed mixture is finished, add about 2 cups B. deliciosa seeds (known by the common name of chocolate chips). Place small amounts of the seed preparation on germination trays, (often called "cookie sheets"), with about 2 inches between each portion.

Put the trays in the oven for 9–12 minutes.

Bake, cool, remove from tray, plant, and water well with a glass of milk.

GREEN JELL-O GARDEN

Utah has the remarkable reputation as the Jell-O Capital of America, particularly lime green Jell-O. During the Winter Olympics in 2002, there was even an Olympic pin offered in the shape of wiggly squares of green Jell-O. Not only is the consumption of Jell-O prodigious, but the many, varied, and unusual items added to Jell-O are interesting in an odd sort of way. The ubiquitous green Jell-O very often accompanies "funeral potatoes" to luncheons and church dinners. Ingredients for this most laughed-about Utah tradition can be found in the Green Jell-O Garden.

Carrots

An ingredient often mixed into the infamous Utah Green Jell-O is bright orange slivers of shredded carrots. Everybody knows carrots are orange, right? Originally, carrots were very light, nearly white—rarely purple or red. In 1689, William III, Prince of Orange of the House of Orange in the Netherlands, invaded and deposed the English King James II. Just like that, the odd orange carrot was cultivated to curry the king's favor. Most of us now accept the orangeness of carrots, but you can also find heirloom as well as modern varieties that are purple, white, red, or yellow. How would your child like green Jell-O with red heart-shaped carrot slices? Or white and purple carrot monster faces staring out from Halloween green Jell-O? You get the idea; think outside the Jell-O box.

Carrot color varies, and so does the recognizable shape and size. They may be long, short, narrow, stubby, pointy like Bugs Bunny favorites, or round like a large marble. But whatever shape, size, or color, those little carrots are not as easily grown as you might think. Carrots befuddle even experienced gardeners. For starters, carrot seeds can take up to three weeks to germinate, and gardeners can lose track of or even give up on the little plants. (See Dig In box.) There are other problems:

PROBLEMS	SOLUTIONS
Heavy or rocky soil will cause carrot roots to contort into what looks like a Boy Scout practice knot.	Your soil needs to be loose and friable (crumbles easily). You will need to add considerable amounts of organic matter to the depth you would like your carrot to grow. If there is no way to get deep soil, or if you are growing in a rather shallow container, select a variety of carrot that grows to be only 2–6 inches long.
If you forget to thin, the carrots can wind together, never reaching full size.	Thin the carrots by snipping off crowded plants right at the level of the soil with a pair of scissors.
Carrot maggots can ruin nearly every little root.	To aid in the prevention of maggots, don't plant carrots in the same place year after year. Practice crop rotation. Cover the carrot crop with floating row cover as soon as the seeds are planted, then remove the cover when the plants are 5–6 inches tall.
Carrot tops can break off when you're trying to harvest the crop.	Dig, rather than pull carrots. Come in from the side of the carrots you intend to harvest with a shovel or spading fork. Loosen the soil, and then they will lift easily from the garden.

Thyme to Dig In

These methods will speed up the carrot germination process and increase success:

 Plant radish seeds right along with the carrot seeds to break up the crust on top of the soil, helping the carrot seeds emerge. The quick-growing radishes also serve as a row marker for the slower-emerging carrots.

 Cover the carrot seeds with sand or vermiculite to keep any crust from forming over the little seeds. Carrots are wimpy little seedlings that can't break through even a slight crust on the soil surface.

 Place a board, plastic, or burlap over the row or block of carrot seeds to hold in the moisture of the soil. After a couple of weeks, peek often so the covering can be removed when the seedlings appear.

 Keep the soil evenly moist as the carrots grow.

VARIOUS COLORS AND TEXTURES OF CABBAGES

ORNAMENTAL CABBAGE

SAVOY-TYPE CABBAGE

Cabbage

Cabbage is a nearly foolproof cool season crop that can be planted early and will survive light frosts. The seedlings can tolerate rather cool temperatures, and the mature "head" is at its best when it finishes growing in cool weather. Cabbage flourishes in fertile, well-drained soil and should be watered often enough to keep the soil moist.

Pick your favorite color because cabbage comes in a choice of green, red, or purple leaves. If you grow the purple type of cabbage, it makes an eye-popping addition to any flowerbed. Leaves can be smooth like Dutch Head cabbage or crinkly if you grow the Savoy types.

If starting plants indoors from seed, begin about six weeks prior to planting outside. Use a floating row cover over the cabbage plants to prevent damage by cabbage loopers, cabbageworms, and aphids. This cover can remain over the cabbage patch all season. During the hottest part of summer, you may need to vent the cover to avoid a buildup of too much heat. Stagger the planting by setting out a plant or two every week for three weeks or plant both early and late varieties at the same time. Do consider that you get one head of cabbage per plant. How much cabbage does your family eat in a week? We suspect 10 heads, even small ones, coming on at the same time may be a little over the limit. Cabbage does store in a refrigerator crisper for a few weeks, but still, a diet of green Jell-O, coleslaw, fish tacos, corned beef, and stuffed cabbage leaves will be tolerated for only so long.

Choose an early short season variety for a harvest of smaller cabbages in the early summer. For longer storage and a second harvest, plant the larger, long season varieties. They can be planted late summer and will mature toward fall. These later large heads can weigh 10 pounds and be 12 inches across; use your pruners to harvest the heavy heads. Then you may want to consider either making sauerkraut or creating a storage area in the basement. Of course, you can let them stay in the garden for quite a while. Pick some as soon as the head is firm when you squeeze it, and let the others continue to grow. As the heads get larger, they may split; harvest as soon as you see the splitting of the outer leaves begin.

Thyme to Dig In

To prevent the heads from splitting, you can root prune the cabbage. Do this by using a shovel on two sides of the cabbage and going straight down into the soil, staying about 4 inches out from the head. Or give the entire cabbage a hard twist to break some of the roots. Root pruning allows you to leave the mature heads in the garden until you are ready to harvest.

Celery

At one time, Utah was a major producer of celery. In the last fifty years, however, most of the fertile rich soil has been paved over for roads, mini-malls, and homes. Utah has a claim on celery production: Tall Utah 52–70 is a variety still recommended and available.

Although it is labor intensive to produce the long, pale stalks of celery that we find in grocery stores, the plants themselves are fairly easy to grow. To get those tender, mild-tasting stalks, most celery needs to be blanched—basically blocking the sunlight from getting to the stalks. The leaves need to be allowed to grow in the sunshine, so don't cover the plant above the top of the stalks. You can use any number of things to blanch: a quart cardboard carton, a length of pipe, a roll of cardboard, or a tall juice can, anything that will hold up to the weather and water and block the sun completely.

If the process of blanching isn't for you, choose to plant a self-blanching variety of celery. You could also choose to just let the celery plants grow willy-nilly as they wish and use mostly the leaves for seasoning in soup, stew, and other dishes.

At least once in your life, you should try loading up that green Jell-O with vegetables out of the garden and serving it for a special occasion—just to say you made and ate what can only be described as a culinary adventure!

Thyme to Dig In

To grow celery:

 Prepare a rich bed *full* of organic matter. The soil needs to stay very moist; consistent moisture is critical if you prefer long stalks to little bushy plants.

 Start your own seeds indoors 8 weeks before the last frost to account for celery's very long growing season. Celery needs light to germinate, so barely cover the tiny seeds. Cover the container with plastic wrap and remove about a week later, after little plants poke up their heads.

Harden off the young plants, and they'll be ready to have their roots plunked into the regular garden soil when nighttime temperatures stay above 45 degrees.

Harvest the leaves anytime once they get a few inches tall. Cut off the entire bunch just above the roots when the blanched stalks get 10 to 12 inches tall, should you be fortunate enough to grow long stalks.

Green Jell-O Salad

1 6-oz. package lime Jell-O
2 cups boiling water

Pour Jell-O powder into a 13 x 9-inch pan.
Add the boiling water and stir until Jell-O is completely dissolved.
Stir in 2 cups ice-cold water.

Add:

1 cup grated carrots
1 cup thinly sliced celery
1 cup finely shredded cabbage

Let set until firm—at least 4 hours.

Cut in squares and serve.

Note: 1 cup canned crushed pineapple may be used in place of the cabbage. Drain well and use the juice as part of the cold water.

FUNERAL POTATO GARDEN

The term "Funeral Potatoes" appears to have originated in Utah. The casserole—made with potatoes, cream sauce, sometimes onions, and then topped with cheese—received its name after frequently being served at Mormon funerals. It too, along with green Jell-O, was featured on a pin at the Salt Lake City 2002 Winter Olympics. A true comfort food, this delectable, don't-count-the-calories dish is served at other social gatherings as well.

There are as many twists to the recipe as there are cooks. But no matter the list of ingredients, we believe freshly dug onions from your own garden add a special zing to the casserole. And while frozen packaged hash browns are used in many recipes, we think nothing is as good as using the real deal—homegrown potatoes. If you have both potatoes and onions, well, there is your Funeral Potato Garden.

Potatoes

"Seed" for potatoes really has nothing to do with seeds—it's actually small potatoes or pieces of larger ones used to get more potatoes! When you buy the seed potatoes, there should be a certificate attesting that those particular potatoes have no diseases. Not that you personally are threatened; the diseases referred to are potato diseases. Potatoes purchased at the grocery store are not certified disease-free and are often treated to inhibit sprouting. We don't recommend using these for seed. Potatoes that spend way too much time in the pantry and sprout long spidery-leg white stems *can* grow in the garden. However, if they do carry any hidden disease, and if that disease is a soil-borne type, you now have a problem for years with potatoes in that part of your garden.

Considerable space is required for potatoes, but containers can also be used. Some folks place fresh potatoes in the same category as homegrown tomatoes—so much better than "store bought" that finding space and making the effort are definitely worth all the worry and work.

Potatoes can go in the ground fairly early in the season. In some areas, St. Patrick's Day is the signal for planting, or for some it is April Fools' Day. Basically, you are looking for the time your soil can be worked after a long winter's wait. Soil that is a sandy loam gives the plants the best chance at large production. The pH should be slightly on the acid side. When soil is too alkaline (high pH, anything over 7) the potato skins become rough or scabby.

Once the gorgeous, crinkled leaves have popped through the soil and the plant is about 9–10 inches tall, you need to start "hilling" the plants. This hilling process helps ensure that sunlight doesn't hit the developing spuds. When sunshine hits the potatoes, a toxic alkaloid is formed and the potatoes turn green. Don't eat the green potatoes!

Potato plants need consistent water, especially once they begin to form the tubers. If the patch really dries out and then gets regular water again, you will have knobby potatoes. Each time the potato dries, it nearly stops growing. But when growth starts up again, does the plant continue to make a bigger potato? Oh, no. It doesn't. It starts another new little potato on the end of the larger one. Interesting shapes form and can be rather like cloud naming—oh, this one looks like a rabbit! Or this one looks more like Dobby the house elf! But even if "name that potato" is a fun game, knobby potatoes are a pain to try to peel or slice.

Around 6–8 weeks after planting, new little potatoes will start forming under the plants. The potato plant starting to flower often heralds this formation. You can choose to harvest the entire plant worth of new potatoes by using a spading fork and digging down at least 12 inches from the center of the plant. Loosen the soil all around the plant and lift the entire kit and caboodle up and out of the soil. This ends potato production for that potato plant, but it should give you a wonderful selection of little new potatoes for steaming, braising, boiling, or mixing with new peas ... yum! To keep the plant producing to the end of the season *and* to enjoy a few new potatoes with your fresh peas, just wiggle your hand down under the soil or mulch and feel for the little roundish potatoes. Gently separate the treasure from the stem it is growing on, and after you are done raiding the patch, firm the soil back lightly and water the area well.

Spacing and Hilling

If all you want is a bumper crop of new little potatoes, you can plant as close as 1 foot between plants. But if you are going for more of a main crop to be harvested later in the season, at least 2 feet should be left between the plants.

The most dreaded chore in the potato patch is usually the job of hilling the potatoes. Like weeding, children are usually assigned to get this part of gardening done. But no matter who volunteers (ha!) or is assigned, hilling needs to be done.

At the end of the growing season, the tops of the plants will turn yellow, then brown, and then die down completely. Frost will speed up this change. Carefully dig up the potato plants—with a spading fork, if possible—and sift through the soil to find the potatoes. It is a near guarantee you will miss some little ones, or even a large one or two, and you will find volunteer potato plants next year. Of course, there is the problem of growing the same plant in the same place too many

HILLED POTATO PLANTS

Thyme to Dig In

A fortunate gardener may find eight or more varieties of potatoes offered at a local nursery. If there is a particular variety that you want for your garden and the nursery doesn't carry it, there are companies that specialize in dozens and dozens of potato varieties: Fingerlings, red, blue, golden, pink, yellow, tiny, extra large, European, Russian, Chilean, ones good for baking, ones good for frying, ones good for boiling, and each can be tracked down with little effort. For baking, try Russet or Kennebec. For boiled, stews, and soups, use Norland or Pontiac. Yukon Gold is a lovely all-around potato that also bakes well. Small, new potatoes are usually best for frying or boiling.

Thyme to Dig In

- Potatoes need full sun (8 or more hours of direct sunshine).
- Planting depths of 4–6 inches is sufficient, or just lay the potato on the ground and cover with 6–8 inches of good mulch or compost.
- Potatoes can be planted in a row, a container, or a "potato tower."
- Cut large seed potatoes into pieces that each have at least two eyes. Allow cut pieces to cure (dry) for a few days before planting. Small, uncut potatoes can be planted whole.

- The hilling process begins when the plants are 8–9 inches tall. To do this, bury the stem with soil or mulch, giving more of the stem a chance to produce your potatoes. Potatoes are a form of modified stem called a tuber. When your plants are sufficiently spaced, you can just pull soil from between the potato plants and pile it up and over the stem and lower leaves. If mulch, like compost or straw, is used to hill the plants, it should be lightweight. Try to leave 3–4 inches of the top leaves uncovered. Repeat two or three times during the season.
- Ease back on the watering when vines begin to yellow.

seasons in a row—best to just yank out the volunteer plants while they're little and you haven't yet gotten attached to them. Gardeners are just not wont to be pulling up something that's lovely, green, and healthy looking, but sometimes it needs to be done.

Onions

"I'm a lonely little Petunia in the Onion patch, the Onion patch, the Onion patch..." Joy's mom used to sing that little ditty, usually as she was dicing onions and had tears streaming down her cheeks. However, those onions were welcome in ever so many yummy foods: fried potatoes, potato salad, Thanksgiving dressing, soup, stew, even with bread and butter and ketchup as a raw onion sandwich—and, of course, a great addition to funeral potatoes.

Onions are undemanding additions to a provident garden. They mix and match well with herbs, flowers, and many vegetables. You can choose one of three ways to add the onion to your gardening repertoire.

1. Directly seed them in the garden.
2. Carefully plant tiny, thin plants you grew in your home or bought from a store.
3. Buy plant sets, which are little dormant onions.

To buy bunches of little plants, head to a full service nursery and garden center or delve into the wonderful world of garden catalogs. A bundle of young plants usually comes in counts of twenty-five or fifty. We don't think that's too many onions, but you can always split the bundle with other gardening friends if that seems like onion inundation.

Most bulb onions seem to grow to a larger size when planted as seed or young plants. But the greater convenience of the little sets will often sway the gardener's choice. Sets are much quicker and easier to plant, and they can be used to produce scallions or bulb onions, depending on how long you let them grow. Balancing against the convenience, though, is the slim pickings as far as the number of different varieties available. In many garden centers, you can buy any onion set you want as long as it is "white," "yellow," or "red." If you do decide on the sets, choose those that are roughly the diameter of a dime. Plant them with the pointy side pointing up and barely poking out of the soil. The larger sets very often think they have already lived a full year, and shortly after they start growing in your garden, they bolt. Onions are biennial, meaning the

first year they stock up on stored energy. This is when they are usually harvested and eaten. The second year, they use that stored food to produce flowers and seeds. Onions that bolt will not get larger and usually have a hollow center where the flower stalk is produced. They are still just fine to eat, but not if you want a big fat slice for onion rings or a topping on your perfect hamburger.

The available onion varieties boggle the mind. Pick your variety, plant many of the seeds in the same pot, and then transfer them to roomier digs when they get about 5–6 inches tall. Do keep the varieties in their own separate containers, if you want to keep records of which varieties you like best. Onions look exactly alike when they start to grow. Even after several weeks, they still all look like skinny little blades of grass. Onion seeds don't store as long as other seeds, so either plant them within a couple of years of purchase or be extra diligent with your storage techniques.

Thyme to Dig In

Sets are usually sold in bags containing dozens of little onion bulbs. Sort through them to group together the dime-sized ones, the larger ones, and finally the itty-bitty ones. Plant each bunch in the same area. The development and harvest of the onions in each group should be similar.

Thyme to Dig In

You'll run into the terms "long day" and "short day" varieties. That refers to the conditions under which an onion is most likely to form the largest bulb. In the southern states and Hawaii, gardeners search out short day varieties. When a cold winter is part of your garden sequence of seasons, long day types work out better. Long day onions start growing when the days are very cool and relatively short. Then as the days lengthen into summer, they begin to put on girth. The short day varieties are usually started in the late summer and like the shorter, cooler days of fall/winter/spring to form the large bulbs. A recently bred combination makes it possible to plant "day neutral" onions that work well wherever you garden. Candy is a lovely, large, white onion that is listed as day neutral.

Onions appreciate a loose, fertile soil. Unlike potatoes, onions prefer a slightly alkaline soil, so the Intermountain West is a super place to enjoy growing onions. They are shallow rooted and need fairly consistent watering. A couple of fertilizer applications a month apart will help develop healthy, green leaves. There must be vigorous top growth to make enough food to create a large bulb.

Deciding when to harvest onions is easy. Any ol' time you want an onion, you can pull one out of the garden. Of course, they will be teeny, skinny, little things if you pull while they are very young, but hey, they are still onions. If you plant onions about an inch apart, as they grow you can thin and partake in one move. Eating the young onion plants as scallions will leave room for the others to beef up and get ready for the hamburger topping later in the season. If you are just interested in nurturing the large bulbs, keep the seeds/sets/plants at least 4 inches apart.

Not everyone loves onions. Some merely tolerate the layered lovelies and some simply can't stand even the aroma. But for others, they are an undeniably essential part of life. A dear friend of Joy's had a grandmother named Noino. The great-grandmother just couldn't get enough onions in every, or any, size, shape, or method of cooking. Hence, when her little girl was born, she was named Noino (No-eye'-no) . . . figured it out yet? Noino is onion spelled backwards!

SPRING ONIONS

Funeral Potatoes (potatoes au gratin)

This wonderful 3-generational recipe from Virginia Timothy is delicious!

9 or 10 large potatoes

1 bunch green onions

1 cube margarine

2 cans cream of chicken soup, undiluted

1 pint sour cream

1½ cups grated cheese*

1 tsp. salt

*extra grated cheese for the top if desired

Boil potatoes in skins and cool. Peel and grate into large mixing bowl. Melt margarine in large frying pan, add onions, and barely brown. Add rest of ingredients and heat thoroughly. Pour sauce over potatoes and mix well. Pour into 9 x 13 pan or dish. Sprinkle extra grated cheese over top. Bake uncovered at 350 degrees for 45 minutes.

THE CINDERELLA-HAD-TO-START-SOMEWHERE GARDEN

Thyme to Dig In

Every autumn brings thoughts of falling leaves, frosty mornings, and fanciful jack-o'-lanterns. The first "lanterns" were actually hollowed out turnips! Now we usually use pumpkins

It takes some advanced planning to grow your own jack-o'-lantern, or Miss Cinderella's Coach if you prefer. You must plant them in the early summer even though you won't harvest pumpkins until the late fall. When planning to grow a perfect pumpkin, it helps to know just what is a pumpkin.

Pumpkins are one of several varieties of winter squash. The winter part of that name refers to the season during which the squash may be stored and then eaten. When ripe (mature), all of these fruits have a thick, hard shell or skin. Sizes can range from a tiny wee 3-inch Jack-Be-Little to a "pumpkin" weighing well over a thousand pounds!

As with all the "warm season" crops, winter squash requires warm soil before planting in the garden. If weather isn't cooperating with the soil warming, the process can be sped up with clear plastic. Before

Thyme to Dig In

- Select an open site with plenty of room that receives full sun.
- Squash prefer soil full of organic matter and that drains well.
- Start seeds indoors 2 weeks before last frost or directly outdoors after soil warms.
- Plant 5–6 seeds in circular hills. Cover with 2 inches of soil.
- Space 4–5 feet apart unless grown vertically.
- Water roots regularly, keeping the stems and leaves dry to prevent disease.
- Harvest after first frost. Leave 2–3 inches of the stem attached to the pumpkin.

Thyme to Dig In

Don't have the space to let a pumpkin vine sprawl all over the ground? Try growing it vertically! Place a trellis in the ground near the base of the pumpkin plant and then gently encourage it upward. Soon those tendrils will take hold, and it will soar toward the sky. And, believe it or not, the vine will thicken and hold the pumpkin in place. If the fruit gets too big and you are worried it will fall, fashion a support out of old nylon stockings or garden netting. Being off the ground will mean a well-shaped fruit without a flattened side from lying on the ground and it's away from the bug. Any vining crop can be grown in this manner.

Winter Squash Varieties

Acorn	Butternut	Kabocha
Banana	Delicata	Pumpkin
Buttercup	Hubbard	Spaghetti

Thyme to Dig In

When a pumpkin is small, scratch a name into the shell. As the pumpkin grows, so will the name. Great for labeling pumpkins for each child in the family.

Thyme to Dig In

If you use soil, mulch, or compost to cover the stem of a winter squash right where a leaf is growing, the vine starts to root there. This adds to the amount of water and nutrients the plant can absorb and helps develop a large harvest.

starting the warm-up, quantities of compost should be added to the soil where the pumpkins will be planted. Then cover the planting area with clear plastic, weighing down the edges with soil, rocks, wood, or maybe bricks.

The area you choose for your pumpkin patch should receive full sun, which will allow the vines to grow vigorously and produce the best harvest of pumpkins. Winter squashes often have a long growing season and do better if planted by starts rather than by seed. These thirsty, hungry plants need regular applications of fertilizer and consistent water. Although the vines scramble across dozens of square feet, it is only around where the vine attaches to the main roots that needs watering and fertilizer. Watering the leaves contributes to and speeds up the inevitable problem of powdery mildew.

Most winter squash can be used interchangeably in different recipes. The one exception might be the Spaghetti Squash because the flesh is rather stringy—hence the use as a vegetable spaghetti. One well-known use for pumpkin is the traditional Thanksgiving pumpkin pie. Sometimes it is disappointing to try a "real" pumpkin to make the pie because it just doesn't taste like the regular one: you know the one—made from canned pumpkin. That canned pumpkin is most often a combination puree of many different kinds of winter squash. A single squash variety just doesn't have the same flavor. But there is just something Cinderella-esque about using a real pumpkin for your family dinner. Besides, whipped cream covers a multitude of flavor differences!

Pumpkin Pie from Scratch
from Karen's Kitchen

Pie Dough:

2 cups flour
1 cup butter-flavored Crisco brand shortening
1 tsp. salt
½ cup tepid water

Mix flour, shortening, and salt with fingers until it resembles a crumb mixture. Add water. Let sit for approximately 15 minutes to make dough easier to work. Dough will be soft—add a tiny bit of flour if too sticky. Roll out to the thickness of a quarter, place in pie tin, and crimp edges.

Makes crust for 4 pies. Excess dough can be frozen in a ball, thawed, and used later.

Pumpkin Pie Filling (for one pie):

2 cups pumpkin puree
1 12-oz. can evaporated milk
2 eggs plus the yolk of a third egg
½ cup packed dark brown sugar
⅓ cup white sugar
½ tsp. salt
2 tsp. cinnamon
1 tsp. ground ginger
¼ tsp. ground nutmeg
¼ tsp. ground cloves

Mix pumpkin, milk, and eggs together. Add sugars, salt, and spices. Mix well.

Pour pie mixture into unbaked shell. Bake on lowest rack of oven at 425 degrees for 15 minutes, then at 350 degrees for 45 minutes.

To make puree: Cut sugar pumpkin, remove seeds, and bake or boil until tender. Cool. Remove pulp and blend until smooth. (Can be frozen and reserved for later.)

THE ROLL-UP-YOUR-WINDOWS-IT'S-ZUCCHINI-SEASON GARDEN

Summer squash, a tasty group of vegetables, gets the name from the fact that they are planted, grown, and harvested in the summer. As a whole squash, they won't store well. They can be frozen, dried, or bottled for use later, but most people favor fresh squash. These varieties of squash also belong to the warm-season vegetable group. Zucchini, et al., should be planted only after the soil is thoroughly warmed. Requiring only a relatively short growing season, you can plant zucchini by seed as well as transplant. When there are at least 70 days—2½ months-ish—remaining before frost, there is time to grow summer squash from seed.

Don't get carried away planting zucchini. Warning: DO NOT plant an entire row of this vegetable. One plant supplies enough for a small family, especially if

> The mere fact that you get a lot of seeds in a packet doesn't mean you have to plant all of them.
> —Henry Mitchell

Summer Squash Varieties

Golden Scalloped

Patty Pan

Zucchini: Eight-Ball, Gold Rush, Black Beauty, Cavili, Bush Baby

Tromboncino

Yellow Crookneck

Yellow Straight Neck

zucchini isn't too high on the favorite vegetable list. On the other hand, if the cook of the house likes to sneak healthy veggies into every dish possible, zucchini is the "grate" pretender. Once grated this humble squash blends into pancakes, muffins, brownies, stews, cookies, casseroles, smoothies, meat loaf, lasagna, chilies, soups, soufflés, cupcakes, spaghetti sauces, breads, stir fry, quiches, and potato pancakes. Joy can keep up with two plants all by herself, since she likes zucchini at least two meals every day. Karen and family usually plant at least four zucchini plants each year—two gold, one black, one green, and sometimes an eight-ball zucchini.

Zucchini's reputation is well-deserved, as many a neighbor can attest who finds yet another paper bag filled with huge zucchini deposited anonymously on the front porch. Or as is often said, "Don't leave your windows down in the church parking lot during zucchini season."

Summer squash, such as zucchini and yellow crookneck, were never intended to be baseball bat stand-ins. Nor were they meant to be garage door propper-uppers, no matter how convenient they seem to be. No, they are meant to be one of the culinary delights coming from your garden. In order for them to be at their tender best, pick zucchini when they are a maximum of six to eight inches long. The baby squash that are so expensive in the store are yours for the picking too. Just snap off any summer squash when they are only 2 to 3 inches long and you'll have a gourmet's delight. (From *Joy in Your Garden*, 33).

Even if you can't keep up with eating, freezing, drying, and sharing all the zucchini, keep them picked so that all the energy in the plant doesn't go to producing those bat-sized clubs. Too-big zucchini is a wonderful addition to the compost pile.

SUMMER SQUASH VARIETIES

Roger van Komen's Best Ever Zucchini Bread

3 cups flour
1 tsp. salt
½ tsp. baking powder
1 tsp. baking soda
¾ tsp. nutmeg
4 tsp. cinnamon
1 cup vegetable oil
2 cups sugar
3 eggs, well beaten
3 tsp. vanilla
3 cups grated zucchini

Combine the flour, salt, baking powder, soda, nutmeg, and cinnamon. Set aside. In another bowl, beat together oil, sugar, eggs, and vanilla. Stir in dry ingredients until well combined. Stir in grated zucchini. Pour into 2 bread pans that have been greased and floured. Bake at 325 degrees for 50 minutes or until done. Cool for 10 minutes before removing from pans. Set on wire racks to cool completely.

Roger van Komen's Chocolate Zucchini Cake

2½ cups flour
½ cup cocoa
2½ tsp. baking powder
1½ tsp. baking soda
1 tsp. salt
1 tsp. cinnamon (optional)
¾ cup butter or margarine
2 cups sugar
3 eggs
2 cups grated, unpeeled zucchini
2 tsp. grated orange peel (optional—½ tsp. of orange extract can be used)

2 tsp. vanilla
½ cup milk
Optional: chopped nuts

Grease and flour 12-cup Bundt pan; set aside. Preheat oven to 350 degrees. In medium bowl, combine first six ingredients; set aside. In large bowl, beat at medium speed the butter with sugar until light and fluffy. Add eggs and beat until well mixed. Stir in zucchini, orange, and vanilla. Alternately stir in dry ingredients, milk, and nuts. Pour into greased pan. Bake one hour or until done. Let cool 10 minutes in pan before turning out onto wire rack to cool. Spread with glaze or chocolate frosting while warm.

FIESTA TACO GARDEN

Some Personal Favorite Tomato Varieties:

Sun Sugar (cherry size)
Delicious
Big Beef
Brandywine (heirloom)
Bart's Best (open pollinated)

At school or at home, vegetarian or some kind of meat, spicy or mild, simple or gourmet, tacos rate high on the list of favorite foods for children of all ages. It is much healthier for all of us when we can control the nutritional value and freshness of ingredients in our own tacos. Who knows? It may spoil your family so much they will only want to eat the home variety. Most families will need to purchase the meat or fish of choice, but many of the other ingredients—tomatoes, peppers, onions, lettuce, and cilantro—can be grown somewhere in your own yard.

And don't stop with a taco—as good as they are. Most of the ingredients for taco salad and salsa are also there in the garden.

Tomatoes

The number one plant grown in the gardens of America is the tomato. Tomatoes come to us from South America via Europe. In Europe they were not always considered edible—possibly because the stems, leaves, and roots are poisonous. Who would have thought that the fruit from a poisonous plant should be put in soup? For some people, the success of the entire gardening season rests on the tomato harvest. Nothing can compensate for failure in the tomato patch. And everyone seems to have their own favorite that they consider the "best" tomato.

With colors from white to near black, red, orange, yellow, green, striped, or speckled, your tomatoes can fulfill your rainbow desire. From half an inch long to weighing 4 pounds and shaped like a pear, torpedo, heart, perfect globe, tear drop, flying saucer, or slightly flattened red softball, or hanging like a cluster of grapes, every tomato is loved by some gardener. There are only minor differences in growing techniques for all of the many and varied forms. Gardeners use basically the same techniques of how to plant, when to plant, when to water, and when to harvest, no matter which variety is grown.

Tomatoes are a warm season plant. Only if you are going to *great* effort to protect them should you consider placing them in the garden before *all* danger of frost has left for the season. On the other hand, you can grow tomatoes in a container and shuttle them in and out of the house for a few weeks before it is safe outside if you have the energy. Where and how is up to you, but the tomatoes need warm air and warm soil.

Containers do more than just let you be the shuttle bus for your tomato. Gardeners with little space can tuck a tomato in anything from a bushel basket to an old wheelbarrow. The container must be put in a place that will receive eight hours or more of direct sunlight. Or you can move the container from the front yard where it gets four hours of morning sun, rolling it around back so the tomato can then take in four hours of afternoon sun. Bothersome? How badly do you crave a fresh homegrown tomato?

Two terms to become familiar with before choosing your yummy taco-topping tomato variety are *determinate* and *indeterminate*. Determinate tomatoes are shorter plants because once the little stems of tomato blossoms are all set (forming tomatoes) that is as tall as the plants will grow. Then most of the tomatoes will ripen at near the same time. Determinate varieties tend to have a shorter growing season and do very well in containers.

Gary Dickson's Fresh Salsa

10 lbs. Roma tomatoes

5 medium-sized Serrano peppers

5 large fresh cloves of garlic

4 bunches of green onions

½ bunch of cilantro

6 medium-sized limes

1 medium-sized purple onion

6 Tbsp. salt

Chop ingredients in a food processor, keeping them as chunky as possible.

Add ingredients one at a time to taste.

If you add too much of one ingredient, add more tomatoes.

Makes 1 gallon. Serve with tortilla chips. Store in refrigerator, but don't expect it to last very long—it will be eaten quickly.

Thyme to Dig In

- Tomatoes should be grown in full sun in well-drained soil, whether they are in a container, a raised bed, or a row.

- Purchase compact plants with sturdy stems. Resist the temptation to buy tall plants that already have small fruit or blossoms.

- Plant stems especially deep, removing any leaves that may end up underground. This will allow for a stronger root system since new roots will form all along the buried stem.

- Plant outside after danger of frost is past. Or, to get an earlier start, provide protection using a Wall o' Water.

- Provide support for the plant as it grows. You can provide support and protection at the same time by making a cylinder of concrete reinforcing screen with 6-inch mesh. Place over the plant and stake into the ground. Provide protection by fastening row cover around the cylinder. (See photo from the garden of Paul Dickson illustrating this.)

- Temperatures above 70 degrees at night or 95 degrees in the day will cause tomatoes to quit setting fruit, even if there are a lot of blossoms. Likewise, too low of temperatures prevent the plant from setting fruit—varying from variety to variety.

- Water regularly and deeply. Avoid overhead irrigation. Reduce water as fruit ripens to prevent splitting.

Indeterminate tomatoes are why gardeners invented 8-foot tall tomato cages. Unless you pinch out the terminal bud (top growing stem), they will grow until frost ends the season. These varieties tend to have a longer growing season and begin to ripen later than the other tomatoes. Many of the giant-sized and heirloom tomatoes are apt to be indeterminate growers. You have been warned. Little 3-foot tomato cages made out of thin wire will bend, topple over, and disappear under the 8-foot avalanche of leaves, vines, and fruit.

Thyme to Dig In

You don't even need a hard-sided container for a tomato. Buy a 2 cubic foot bag of really good potting soil. Put that down where there are 8 hours of direct sun—it doesn't matter if it is on the deck, sidewalk, patio, or even in the middle of the lawn. As long as you poked several holes in the underside of the bag, you can plant one or two tomato plants right in the bag. Cut a "T" or an "X" in the topside of the bag and make room for the tomato roots. Plant it as deeply as you can. The more stem under the surface the better. Remember to strip the leaves from the part of the stem that will be buried in the potting soil.

Peppers

Peppers, sweet or hot, are relatives to the tomato. Many of the same growing techniques and conditions that make tomatoes happy will make peppers happy. Peppers do *demand* warm, warm soil. They will pout and become stunted if they are put into garden soil that hasn't really warmed up. Try for a soil temperature of at least 70 degrees. Peppers also have a narrow range of temperatures in which they will set fruit. If peppers lived in a pepper perfect world, temperatures would be 90 degrees during the day and close to 70 degrees at night.

If you live in an area where the summer temperatures soar above 90 degrees for many consecutive days, you may want to create a bit of a sunscreen over your pepper plants as the blossoms start to form. One Master Gardener uses his 5–6-foot-tall tomato plants to create shade for his shorter peppers. He plants the peppers on the east side of his tomatoes. Later he builds a PVC pipe frame over the peppers and covers it with a lightweight frost blanket to prevent sunscald of the fruit.

Peppers incorporated into an ornamental flowerbed can be positioned to get the same kind of shade, perhaps from a tall rose or short shrub, like the lovely Siberian pea shrub. The flowers and ripening fruit of peppers are gorgeous when combined with low blue flowers like lobelia or ageratum. They also get along well with bright yellow or orange marigolds.

Thyme to Dig In

All peppers turn from green to other colors if left to ripen on the plant.

You can put mild or searingly hot peppers directly on your taco, in with the meat preparation, or added to tomatoes and onions to create a salsa that will top the finished product. Before cutting the peppers from the plant, you may choose to wait until the lovely yellow, red, or orange color develops, rather than the usual green color. But do *cut* the stem of the pepper instead of just yanking it off. Pepper stems are fairly small and can be broken easily. Once broken off, there ends the pepper production for that stem.

Lettuce

Lettuce germinates in a matter of days, can be eaten a few days later, and is finished producing within weeks. But this is no flash in the salad bowl vegetable. It has staying power even for those few weeks because it can be harvested every day and still provide the basis for a salad the next day. The trick is to just snip off the outer leaves to use for your meal. The center leaves continue to multiply, and this can go on and on until either it gets too hot, causing the lettuce to bolt, or you need the space in the garden for other summer veggies.

Lettuce is really mostly water and must grow in consistently lightly moist soil. It also needs cool temperatures to do well. This means plant early in the season and keep the water coming. Allowing the soil to dry not only slows the growth but also often makes the lettuce leaves very bitter.

It's possible to let lettuce masquerade as a perennial instead of an annual. Let one or two, or more, of the

Thyme to Dig In

In 1912, Wilber Scoville developed a test to determine how hot a pepper is perceived to taste. An extract of the pepper is taken and diluted in sugar water until it no longer can be detected as "hot." It is the chemical compound capsaicin that stimulates the nerves in the tongue and tells the brain that it's hot. A sweet green pepper has a Scoville rating of zero. Granted, this is a subjective rating, dependent upon the testers who rated the pepper. But it does give a relative idea of heat, and that may change your mind when you are deciding which HOT pepper to plant.

Name	Scoville Units
Naga Jolokia	855,000+
Habanero	350,000+
Jamaican	125,000
Thai	100,000
Tabasco	50,000
Serrano	25,000
Jalapeño	8,000
Ancho	2,000
Anaheim	1,000
Pepperoncini	500
Bell pepper	0

lettuce plants go to seed. You might be surprised at what a tall attractive plant lettuce can be when in bloom. It has a tapered "Christmas Tree" shape with cute little yellow flowers. The seeds are carried throughout your garden by little white parachutes. Next season there will be young lettuce plants popping up all over the garden. Let them grow for a while even if they are in the wrong—let that read "unplanned"—place in the garden. After a couple of weeks, you can remove them and add the unplanned lettuce to an early spring salad.

Thyme to Dig In

Plant a second crop of lettuce in early August for a fall crop. The seeds will germinate quickly in the warm soil and the leaves will flourish in the cool autumn temperatures. You will be able to enjoy that fresh "spring" lettuce all over again!

Cilantro

The herb of choice for tacos, salsa, and any number of Latin dishes receives a mixed review from us. One of us likes to smell it and thinks you can't use too much in cooking. The other of us would rather not, thinking it smells and tastes like soap. But should you, in spite of that warning, come down on the side of Viva Cilantro, know that it suffers from MND—that is, Multiple Name Disorder.

- Cilantro—a leafy addition to salads and so on, especially in Latino dishes.

- Chinese Parsley—a leafy addition to many oriental dishes.

- Coriander—seeds of a leafy plant, the seeds being used in sweet confections as well as savory dishes.

Ah-ha! Those are all the same herb! Well, leaves and seeds of the same herb. You will find little seed packets on the same rack with each name on a different packet. The seeds inside are identical. But people out to grow cilantro are not about to pick up a packet of coriander seed. Likewise, those looking for Chinese parsley seeds to grow in their garden will not buy cilantro seeds. So each packet gets a different name and goes home with a satisfied gardener to produce "different" plants used in different foods.

By any name, cilantro is a horrible tease—luring gardeners into believing they too can grow cilantro. Ha. It isn't the growing that is the difficulty; it is the timing of the harvest that doesn't work out. When would most of us like to have a large bunch of cilantro? Probably when the tomatoes, onions, and peppers are ripe and ready to be chopped for fresh salsa. When is cilantro ready for harvest? About 3 weeks after it's planted, and that probably means about May. Then within a day or two it has bolted and gone to coriander.

Unless you live somewhere that approximates the growing conditions on the Yucatan Peninsula, it is far easier to pick your cilantro at the local grocery store than it is to grow your own. If it is too cool after the cilantro germinates and starts to grow, it bolts. If it is too hot after the cilantro germinates and starts to grow, it bolts. So plant early, and cilantro bolts. Wait and plant later, and cilantro bolts. Good luck.

HEAVEN SCENT GARDEN

Joy's favorite scent and flavor in the garden is lemon, and that includes her 4-foot tall Meyer lemon tree! Of course, the tree joins her in the house during the winter months, bringing with it the sweet fragrance of lemon blossoms during the white winter season. Out in her garden, it is the lemon-scented herbs that carry on the lovely scent.

Lemon verbena, lemongrass, and lemon basil are annuals and must be replanted each year, but it is well worth the extra effort. As perennials, both lemon balm and lemon thyme return to the garden on their own, with gusto! Besides a lemon-scented garden, you can choose from many, many other themes to create a heavenly scented area.

Make the most of the superb quality of herbs to release fragrance into the garden. By placing herbs along paths in your garden, you and others can gently stroke the leaves as you walk by. Herbs in containers should be within reach. Most herbs must be ruffled a bit to release the fragrant essential oils contained in the leaves. These plants are made for petting!

Thyme to Dig In

The informal, but grouped together, herb garden is a natural place to develop a theme garden. You can select herbs, for instance, that are mentioned in Shakespeare as a Shakespeare Garden, or herbs with biblical references as an Old or New Testament Garden. Grandparents may want to combine story time with books by Beatrix Potter with their gardens. They can read to their grandchildren and then take a stroll out in the garden to find the vegetables that Peter Rabbit ate or guide the kids to the chamomile that Mrs. Rabbit used to make tea that settled Peter's tummy.

Choose your favorite author and search for the herbs used in their writings:

Shakespeare
Bay laurel
Burnet
Fennel
Hyssop
Lavender
Marjoram
Mint
Parsley
Thyme

Beatrix Potter's Peter Rabbit
Calendula
Chamomile
Nasturtium
Parsley
Rose

Become a history buff and create your own herb time machine to transport your garden back into history:

Colonial Herbs
Anise
Basil
Coriander
Dill
Chives
Sage
Thyme

HERB GARDEN ON A PATIO

Herbs need not be placed in a separate, formal garden of their own. They mingle and play well with others. Of course, if you lean toward the formal look, it is difficult to imagine a more classic look than a well-trimmed, symmetrically-planted herb garden.

Many of our most familiar herbs originally grew in the Mediterranean area. They enjoy hot, dry summers, soil that drains well but is not particularly nutrient rich, and precipitation that is concentrated mainly in fall and spring. If your garden has heavy soil that retains moisture, especially during the winter months, there will be no end of problems for plants like lavender and rosemary. Without soil that drains well, they suffer from crown or root rot. For gardeners without near- perfect drainage, try raised beds or containers.

In fact, nearly every herb will do well in pots and containers of all sizes and shapes. Just be sure each container has good drainage out the bottom. Plant a single herb in a single pot or several individual plants of the same herb in a large container. Perhaps you would like a window box—fill it with several different herbs and put the box outside your kitchen window to be handy when you want to snip fresh herbs for that spaghetti sauce or omelet. Get to know new herbs that you haven't grown before. Choose some for use in the kitchen, some for fragrance, and some just because they are beautiful plants!

Here are a few uncommonly delightful common herbs to get the ideas flowing.

Basil

Basil is an annual herb with many named varieties. This herb is easy to grow from seed and can be planted by seed directly in the garden once the soil  has warmed. It will do best in full sun. Basil may be grown in containers but probably should be replanted every three weeks or so since the plants quickly get long and leggy without sufficient light. Tomato plants seem to grow better when grown near basil, which is right handy when it's time to pick the makings of pizza sauce! You may find purple basil, including purple ruffles, in your local nursery. It is a whiz-bang addition to a flowerbed. As either an accent or a border, purple basil is a real eye-catcher. Basil leaves are used in cooking. They will turn black in the fridge, so if you pick several stems, place them in a glass of water like you would fresh flowers. They stay fresh for a couple of days, and you can pick the leaves as needed for your recipes.

Chives

Chives poke their oniony leaves out of the ground very early each spring. As one of the perennial herbs, chives can double as a lovely spring flower and a topping for your baked potato or omelet. The leaves are thin and tubular. The stem holding up the flower is also tubular, but don't try using it in cooking. The flower stem is tasteless and rather like a woody stem of straw. The little cluster of lavender flowers are edible, however. Take each individual little flower

CHIVE FLOWER

GARLIC CHIVE FLOWER

from the ball of florets and sprinkle them on cream soup or a salad. Be advised that the leaves may have a mild onion flavor, but the cute little flowers have a hot little zing to them. Chives can end up all over your garden if you let seeds form. Each of those little florets will form a small black seed. A flower head may have a couple dozen or more florets. And every little black seed will germinate. To keep the chives in control, just pull off the spent flowers before they go to seed. If you want just a couple of new chive plants, it is very easy to divide the plant. Each stem ends in a tiny, green, onion-looking plant. Cut or tear the clump apart, and you'll have two or many new chive plants.

Spring bulbs and chives make a beautiful color combination in your spring garden. And they work as a nice informal hedge along a path. They die down to the ground every year, so they need very little maintenance. Garlic or Chinese chives are similar plants but have flat leaves and loose clusters of white florets. You'll find them blooming in the late summer instead of spring. And these chives do

have a slight garlic flavor combined with the onion taste. Be careful, they can become weedy, meaning that once seeds scatter and start growing they are difficult to pull.

Harvest chives while young and tender and use when fresh. The long leaves can also be cut up, dried, and stored in a jar for later use. Another alternative is to freeze freshly cut-up chives in small packets to add to a savory dish when needed.

Oregano

Oregano is a cousin in the mint family. This perennial herb is probably best recognized as the "pizza herb." This herb enriches any and all

tomato-based sauces. It does have the family tendency to encroach on the area around where it is growing. Given an inch, it will take over your yard. But it is easy to pull up, so we don't think it slips into the weedy category. Oregano lineage is difficult to trace and really gets mixed up if it is grown from seed. Many generic oregano plants are labeled Greek oregano but are missing the spicy depth of flavor that real Greek oregano is known for. Try nibbling a small piece of leaf before you believe the label. What are you looking for? It should bite back! Golden oregano is milder, in both flavor and tendency to ramble. Any of the oreganos can make a tall ground cover; or they can be kept trimmed back to 4–5 inches tall. But if you trim consistently to keep them short, you will miss the lovely small stalks of blue flowers. And bees and other pollinators will lose one of their favorite pollen-gathering stations.

Lavender

Lavender is a bushy perennial herb that loves it hot and dry. Lavender does require excellent drainage with no organic mulch near the crown, or stem, of the plant. It is grown primarily for the lovely wands of lavender-colored flowers (what else?), and the grayish leaves are also very fragrant. You can find several flower colors—some are darker purple, pink, or white. Lavender is a lovely choice if you are looking for a small, formal, or informal hedge. Prune back by half after the early summer flowers fade, and you'll probably be rewarded with re-bloom later in the season. This herb is favored by the British for soap, potpourri, and lotion. If you like to make dried flower arrangements or crafty thingies, lavender is simple to dry. Cut the flower stalks just as the first little flowers are opening. Tie a handful of stems together and hang them upside down. Make sure they are in an area that gets excellent

warm air circulation. If you have an attic, that could be a good place to dry herbs. Tie a small paper sack over the flower end of the bundle if you want to ensure saving every little flower.

Parsley

Parsley is a biennial. That is true of both the flat leaf and curled leaf varieties of parsley. For some people, the first introduction to parsley

came when a meal was served with a ruffly sprig of green stuff on the side. "Eat it," your mom said. "It's good for you (or your breath)." But even before that encounter, you probably tasted parsley and

didn't even know it. Chopped parsley is called for in many homemade soups, salads, salsas, and stews. Noted chefs prefer the flat leaf variety, but both kinds are used in many recipes interchangeably. As a biennial, parsley forms a dense group of leaves in the first season. The second year it sends up a flower stalk that looks very much like a carrot flower. Yes, they are related. If parsley seed is allowed to scatter about the garden, the following spring you will find delightful emerald green tufts of parsley growing in random areas. Fine idea, but if it happens to be in a spot where you don't want parsley to grow, you better pull them while the plants are very little. The taproot grows quickly and makes it much harder to pull as the plant grows larger. Parsley loves full sun but will grow in partial shade as well. It needs only a medium amount of water, so it does well among flowers in the ornamental garden. In fact, it is a gorgeous border plant for one season plus the next spring. Then, in the early summer of its second year, parsley throws up the flower stalk and dies, but not right away. It dies a yellowing, lingering death after the seeds are formed. You may not want to put parsley in an important focal place in the front garden.

Sage

Sage is the herb often thought of when remembering Grandma's Thanksgiving dressing. It is a very easy herb to grow, requiring only lots of sun and fair drainage. The usual sage plant has dusty gray-green leaves and woody stems. The leaves are rather leathery and thick. When used in cooking, whole leaves should be removed from the food before serving. Usually

the leaves are dried and then ground finely. The dried form is much more pungent than the fresh leaves. You can flavor chicken and turkey by sliding the sage leaves between the skin and the meat just before cooking.

Sage really deserves to be planted for more than the makings of turkey stuffing. There are other varieties of sage that make a great ornamental splash in a sunny garden. Golden sage has wide margins on each leaf that are golden green in color. The more sun, the brighter the edges will appear. Purple sage has a slight purple tint to the upper side of the leaves, while the undersides are deep purple. One of the favorite sages for ornamental use is the Tricolor sage. Again, the leaves have colored margins, but these colors are creamy white and pink with a gray-green middle. In addition to the lovely colors, these different varieties also have the tendency to grow more slowly and get less woody over the years. As a large plant, 2 to 3 feet wide and tall, they are a splashy anchor plant in an herb garden, vegetable patch, or flowerbed.

Rosemary

Rosemary shows up around Christmastime in a little sheared tree form, usually with a nice red bow on top. In most catalogs, rosemary is listed as a perennial. Once taken home, it can quickly become a tree-shaped mass of dead needle leaves. Sad to say, most of the plants are doomed to quick crispiness during the holiday season. Unlike most other "house" plants, rosemary plants won't recover from wilting. So once dry, they are permanently dry. They also will not tolerate the hot dry whoosh of forced  air heating, plus they really need a lot of bright sunlight. All in all, holiday homes are far from hospitable places for rosemary plants.

But nothing can come close to the piney pungent aroma of fresh rosemary leaves. So what is a gardener or cook to do? From Zone 5 to 10 the answer is to grow the plant outside! As an evergreen, the leaves and stems are available even in the winter. Just brush off the snow, and there is the lovely ingredient for rosemary chicken! If you live at the edge of rosemary's hardiness—that is to say Zone 5—you need to look for the variety called Arp. We've found it to be the most reliably hardy in this zone. The rather odd variety name comes from the town in Texas where the gentleman who developed the variety lived. One further note: in the cooler zones, rosemary should be planted in the late spring or early summer so it can develop good roots before facing a cold winter.

Thyme

Thyme is a perennial herb with tiny leaves. The young stems and leaves are chopped and added right to the food, but older  stems should be stripped and only the little leaves used. Or cut stems about 4–5 inches long and place them in the cooking food, just a few minutes before serving. Remember to remove the stems before eating. English thyme is the variety with the most recognizable "thyme" fragrance and taste. It is a small evergreen plant, 10–12 inches tall, and fits nicely in the veggie, herb, or ornamental garden. Creeping thyme, a wonderful ground cover, may have a regular thyme aroma or be lemon, nutmeg, lime, or orange scented. These small creeping plants make a thick ground cover. Elfin thyme gets no more than a half inch tall and fills in between stepping-stones beautifully. Doone Valley creeping thyme is covered with bright pink flowers during bloom time and is then a low, mounding plant that gets about 4–6 inches tall for the rest of the season. Doone Valley leaves are variegated with cream-colored edges, adding another dimension to its beauty. All creeping thyme plants enlarge slowly, covering maybe 2 feet square when they are mature.

At this point, gardeners of a certain vintage will probably be humming or even singing out loud "Parsley, sage, rosemary, and thyme . . ." This is a most reasonable reaction to the listing of the above four herbs.

Mint

Mint is a perennial herb so rampant in its growth that it is sometimes termed invasive. Most herbs like full sun, but mint actually prefers some shade. Mint sends out both under- and above-ground stems as well as creeping roots. Be sure you really want mint in the area where you are considering planting it. It flourishes in moist soil, so a dry area will help keep the spreading in check. Now, with that caution out of the way, we think mint is super, even growing in the lawn! But should you think that is going a little—or a lot—too

Super-Duper Chocolate Mint Sundae

Scoops of your favorite chocolate ice cream
Mint syrup
Whipped cream
Slivered almonds
Maraschino cherries
Scoop the ice cream, drizzle with cold mint syrup, and pile on the whipped cream. Top with nuts and a cherry.

Mint Syrup

1 cup water
1 cup white sugar
½ cup fresh mint leaves, preferably spearmint.

Combine sugar and water, heat until sugar dissolves and then boil for 1 minute. Set aside.

Scrunch the mint leaves into a measuring cup and then place them in a pint jar (or similar heat proof container).

*Muddle thoroughly.

Pour hot syrup over the muddled mint leaves and let steep. Thirty minutes is about right, but you may want to experiment to find out how strong you want the mint flavor to be.

Allow the mint syrup to cool until just warm. Strain out the mint leaves.

Place the jar in refrigerator until needed for the sundae.

This syrup will keep for weeks in the fridge.

*Muddle: Mash with a Muddler.** Or use the end of a wooden spoon to mash the leaves.

**Muddler: A bartender's tool, used like a pestle to mash fruits, herbs, and/or spices in the bottom of a glass to release their flavor.

far, a container of mint might be just right for you. Mint in containers can be placed almost anywhere and tolerates nearly any condition except full, hot sun. Even when it is neglected—let that read "forgot to water for two weeks"—a thorough watering will bring it back to its minty fresh best. You can find the two major groups of mint—spearmint and peppermint—in most nursery and garden centers. A potted mint collection could contain peppermint, spearmint, orange mint, apple mint, lime mint, chocolate mint, and pineapple mint. A little searching in a good catalog will add at least twenty more varieties to the list.

Saffron

Besides the delightfully common basil, oregano, chives, sage, thyme, and so on, there is also an uncommon little plant that produces the most expensive herb (or spice) in the world. And this plant does quite well in most of our local gardens. This

SAFFRON CROCUS

SAFFRON THREAD

extremely expensive spice is saffron. Saffron is treasured the world over, both for the rich flavor and the brilliant color it imparts to food. Saffron is the tiny stamen of the fall blooming crocus, Crocus sativa. Each little flower, which blooms like an amethyst jewel in late fall, supplies only three tiny stamen about the size of a ½-inch piece of heavy thread. These saffron threads must then be dried before using. Although it requires literally millions of the tiny purple flowers to provide the world with enough saffron for a single year's use, with twenty or so of the corms, you can grow enough stamen to provide sufficient use for two or three favorite recipes.

Good as Gold Saffron Lemon Bread

¼ tsp. saffron threads
½ cup cold butter
¾ cup sugar
2 eggs
Grated zest of 1 lemon
2 cups white flour, unbleached
½ tsp. salt
2 tsp. baking powder
2 tsp. fresh lemon juice
¾ cup water

Use two spoons to grind or powder saffron. (The threads are the little stamen from the Saffron crocus. See above.) Mix the powdered saffron into the cold butter. Mix until evenly distributed. Cream the saffron butter with the sugar. Add the eggs, one at a time. Add the lemon zest. In another bowl, sift together the dry ingredients. Combine water and lemon juice.

Add a little of the water mixture to the creamed ingredients. Add about ⅓ of the dry ingredients; mix lightly. Continue to alternate the dry ingredients with the water. DO NOT OVERMIX. Batter will be thick.

Preheat oven to 350 degrees. Pour batter into greased, floured bread pan or muffin tins. Bake loaf for about 50 minutes; muffins take about 25 minutes. The loaf should be just lightly browned and beginning to pull away from the edges.

Cool for 10 minutes, then turn out of the pan and onto a rack to cool.

Not all fall-blooming crocus are saffron crocus. Be sure you buy only Crocus sativa if you want to grow this "living gold." The plants need eight hours or more of direct sunshine, well-drained soil, and an appreciative audience. It takes only a steady hand to harvest the saffron. When the flowers are in full bloom, carefully pull out the brilliant red-orange stamen from the center of the flower. Place them between two layers of paper towel and let dry in a warm place for at least a week. The long, grasslike leaves should be left to grow until the next spring, when they will dry out and can be removed from the garden.

Surprise Rosemary Bars

2 large eggs, beaten well
$2/3$ cup soft dark brown sugar
$1\frac{1}{2}$ tsp. vanilla
1 cup flour
$\frac{1}{2}$ tsp. salt
1 tsp. baking powder
1 Tbsp. finely minced fresh rosemary
8 oz. raisins and/or candied fruit such as citron

Preheat oven 375 degrees.

An 8 x 8 inch pan works best.

Combine the first three ingredients and beat well. Sift together the three dry ingredients. Stir the dry ingredients into the moist ingredients. Batter will be very stiff. Fold in rosemary, raisins, and candied fruit. Dried currants work best for the raisins.

Drop by large spoonfuls in the pan and smooth the batter as much as possible.

Bake for 30 minutes. Bars will be lightly browned and will pull away from the edge of the pan.

Cool slightly before cutting into bars. Finish cooling on a rack. Makes 20–24 bars.

Thyme for Lemon Shortbread

$\frac{1}{2}$ cup plus 1 Tbsp. butter
$\frac{1}{4}$ cup confectioners' sugar
1 tsp. lemon zest
3 tsp. minced fresh lemon thyme
$1\frac{3}{8}$ cups flour
Extra confectioners' sugar

Preheat oven 350 degrees.

Cream first two ingredients by hand until very smooth. Add the fresh lemon zest and thyme. Add flour very gradually, you may not need it all. Mix together to make a very soft dough. Wrap in plastic wrap and chill for about an hour.

Roll the dough on a lightly floured surface until about $3/8$ inch thick. Cut into rectangles. Place on a greased cookie sheet. Bake for 15–18 minutes.

DON'T OVERBAKE. Cool for 2 minutes and then remove to rack and dust lightly with confectioners' sugar.

FAQs

Can you buy carrot transplants?
No, the little plants need to develop in the soil where they will be growing. Carrots are big tap roots, and tap roots don't like to be moved. If you are very, very careful you can try moving some of the tiny seedlings to a row next to the original one. A few of them might make it.

Can you eat weeds?
Some plants that we call weeds, other folks delight in eating as salad greens. Dandelion leaves herald the end of winter, and people for ages looked forward to eating the young leaves. The flowers can be used to make dandelion wine. This lowly purslane makes a tangy addition to soups and salads. It contains protein, vitamins E and C, and Omega 3 fatty acids. And it's free and plentiful! Before eating, make sure someone hasn't sprayed it with a little broad-leaf weed killer.

What fertilizer does a cabbage plant need?
Good compost-rich soil is the best fertilizer. A foliar application of an organic fertilizer, like seaweed extract, every couple of weeks is a good addition. If you use chemical fertilizer, choose one that has potassium and phosphorus as well as nitrogen.

Do onions and garlic really repel pests?
Stories abound touting the amazing results using members of the onion family to protect garden plants. These have some basis in fact, but you certainly can't count on having zero insect problems if you plant garlic around your roses, for instance. Intermixing different flowers, vegetables, and herbs is a good idea to confuse the damaging insects and feed the predators. Besides, garlic, onions, and chives look pretty around roses! And they also look good scattered among the other plants as well. One pest that certainly doesn't like the onion family is the deer that might be in your area. Ornamental onions that grow 2 to 3 feet tall would be a good choice for planting between the deer path and your garden.

How long can potatoes stay in the ground?
Potatoes are usually lifted before the ground freezes solid. Frozen potatoes go mushy. Most home potato growers know that somehow little potatoes that weren't harvested one year grow into potato plants the next year. For ease of digging and surety of harvest, try to dig your crop before the ground freezes.

Can you save onion seeds?
Onions are biennials, so you need to wait until the second season before the onion will flower and set seed. Saving seed is a good idea, but since the seeds lose viability quickly, it is best to use fresh seed every year.

Why do onions make your eyes water?
Onion cells contain chemicals containing sulfur. Enzymes that were separated from those chemicals are released when you cut into an onion. A volatile sulfur compound is formed as the enzyme interacts with the released sulfenic acid. This gas drifts up and reacts with the tears in your eyes, creating sulfuric acid that burns the eye, thus causing more tears to form to wash out the irritant. Chilling the onion slows the enzyme reaction, reducing the gas formed. Cutting the onion while it is under water nearly stops the painful tearing.

How do I treat powdery mildew on my squash leaves?
Fungal infections are best treated with prevention. Once the spores land and grow into the leaves, there

isn't much you can do. Neem oil sprayed weekly on the leaves is one treatment. Or you can mix up a batch of homemade spray: 1 gallon of water, 1 tablespoon of baking soda, 1 tablespoon of dish soap, and 1 tablespoon of vegetable oil (canola recommended). Mix well and apply weekly with a spray bottle. Recent studies have shown that powdery mildew prefers cool (60 to 80 degree) temperatures and dry conditions to spread. It is suggested that a simple daily fine spray of water on the leaves may prevent and control the disease. Don't let the leaves be wet going into the night—that may open the door to other types of fungal problems.

What causes the black spot on the bottom of my tomatoes?

The leathery black or brown bottom of the tomatoes is called "blossom-end rot" and is most often seen on the first fruits of the season. The cause is thought to be a calcium deficiency caused by the plants not having enough water to draw from the soil, especially during the nighttime hours. The way to avoid this problem is to keep the soil moisture consistent by using an organic mulch 3–4 inches deep or a woven plastic mulch. The top side of your tomato is fine to eat, but by the time you cut off the leathery bottom ,there usually isn't too much left! Later in the season the roots have extended into more soil, and they are likely to find enough moisture to keep the problem from occurring.

Why don't my tomato plants have any tomatoes?

Way too much fertilizer, especially nitrogen fertilizer, will encourage only leaf production. If the plants are near a lawn area, the nitrogen used to keep the lawn super green may be hitting the tomato plants as well. Tomatoes need full sun, and if grown in a shady area may not produce fruit. Or it could just be that you chose a long season tomato that doesn't have time to set fruit in your area before the frost hits.

Why is my lettuce bitter?

As a cool season crop, lettuce starts fast, grows fast, and sets seed fast. If hot temperatures start before you can harvest the lettuce, the leaves most often turn bitter. The heat also speeds up the maturation process, and when mature, lettuce plants bolt. This bolting also causes the leaves to be bitter. Not enough water may also be the cause of bitter lettuce. The fast growth and thin leaves require even and constant moist soil. Gardeners can control these conditions by planting early, watering and fertilizing often, and mulching with a deep layer of compost.

Can I bring my herbs inside from the garden?

If they have been growing in containers, you can bring them inside. Most herbs need bright sunlight and won't grow well indoors. But you can continue har-

BASIL

vesting for quite a while. Then cut the plants back by about half and put them in the brightest location you have. Warning: there may be little hitchhikers on the plants. Insects that were no problem outside will multiply greatly and may not only kill the herb but spread to your houseplants as well. Since you may be eating the herbs, be careful what you use to get rid of the pests. Neem oil or insecticidal soap sprayed on both sides of the leaves and the stems can be used. Then wash the leaves again with plain water the next day.

Can you eat scented geraniums?

You can use the leaves to impart flavor to jellies, cakes, biscuits, and other foods. The leaves aren't eaten but are removed before serving the dish. You could chop the leaves very finely and mix them with butter and other herbs to use on meat, bread, and so forth. The leaves are tough, rough, and best not chewed—"yuck" is the usual description of the chewed leaves.

When do I thin my peaches?

Pruning begins the thinning process. The next step is taken when the little peaches are about the size of an almond. This is about the time of the normal June drop when the incompletely pollinated fruit will fall from the tree. If you grab a branch and shake it vigorously, you can aid this process. Remove the "twinners," or the little double fruit. Twist, don't pull, the fruit off the branch. Take off the peaches nearest the ends of the branches, then leave about 6 to 8 inches between the remaining fruit.

When do I harvest my herbs?

Early in the morning, just after the dew has dried. The flavor in the leaves will be strongest before the plants flower.

Do blue potatoes stay blue when you cook them?

Nope. They turn a rather unappetizing grayish color.

I've heard tomatoes love to grow with basil— is this true?

This combination has proven to be beneficial to both plants. Grow a row of basil next to or in between your tomato plants. There will be fewer insect problems and better growth.

Can I eat the mushrooms growing in my lawn?

NO! NO! And don't let the kids try them either.

Chapter 3: From Seeds to Plants and Back Again

In the beginning, seeds did originally come *from* the flowers of plants, not from packets purchased at a store or through a catalog. Most of the seeds we plant today come *out* of packets. Although you can spend four dollars for eight special tomato seeds, mostly you can get scads of seeds for somewhere between one and four dollars per packet. Usually on the back of the little envelope is a chart telling you important information, including the length of row that can be planted using all the seeds. That advice, along with other helpful ideas, is often ignored. That is sort of an aggressive word: *ignored*. Most of the time, gardeners don't even notice that there is information *on* the back of the packet.

After all, you've marked out the area in the garden ready for planting. Don't you just keep shaking out seeds until the packet is empty? You don't? Then what do you do with the leftover seeds? Now, be careful that you don't put them in *a safe place*. A safe place is where car keys, five-dollar bills, passports, special Christmas ornaments, birthday presents bought a month early, fancy scissors, combination padlocks (or the combination to the lock), and instruction manuals for whatever just broke down go to hide forever. Okay, not forever. Just until you can buy a replacement, then poof! They are right where you left them. Right, indeed!

> Optimism is the faith that leads to achievement. Nothing can be done without hope and confidence.
> —Helen Keller

You should know that the seeds you buy from seed dealers are ready for storage. That means they are completely dry. It also means the package still has the plant name and the instructions and information pertinent for that plant—you know, all the information that would have been helpful the first time you planted some of those seeds. Stuff like germination rate and planting dates. Should you be worried that it has been three weeks without a sign of little green things coming up? Or maybe you realize something was planted early when it should have waited for June—no wonder it froze.

> Every year it seems to me I hear complaints about spring. It is either "late" or "unusually cold," "abnormally dry" or "fantastically wet," for no one is ever willing to admit that there is no such thing as a normal spring. —Thalassa Crusso

The leftover seeds should be kept in the package and then stored in a cool, dark, dry place. If you put the seed packets in a fairly airtight container, they will stay viable for years. There you go! No need to buy packet after packet of zucchini seeds because you chucked the thirty-one extra seeds from last year's packet. After all, nobody would plant that many zucchini seeds in one season. Would they? Hmmm . . . well, they would only do it once, right?

HYBRIDS

Let's share a quick word of explanation about hybrid varieties of vegetables. There is a phrase used by gardeners: "comes true to seed." That means the fruit from the seed will be the same as the fruit that produced the seed. In other words, you get just what you were expecting from the garden. But if you save the seeds from that hybrid fruit, the results the next year may be far from what you thought you were planting. A simplified explanation goes something like this:

To get a large, tasty tomato that grows on a disease-resistant plant, hybridizers may have used as a daddy tomato a big burly plant even though the tomatoes were small and nearly tasteless. Then for a mama tomato they chose one of the most delicious tomatoes ever found, but the poor plant was puny and prone to several diseases. When the cross is made between mama and daddy tomato—shazzam! The result is a big, tasty tomato growing on a sturdy, disease-free plant. Super success is declared and everyone lines up to buy seeds for that hybrid. However, when the seeds from the fruit of that super successful tomato are planted the next year, up pops plants like daddy or mama or maybe even grandma pear tomato. You just never know what the roll of the genetic dice will bring to the garden—the seeds just don't come true.

Hybrids have all the vigor and disease resistance that comes from their breeding. They may end up being your absolute favorite variety and you want to keep growing them, either from starting your own seedlings or directly sowing the hybrid seeds right in the garden. It will be best if you buy extra packets of the seeds and store them for years to come. That way you know that the first generation of plants will be just what you wanted.

To get produce that "comes true to seed," you need to look for open-pollinated varieties. That way, no matter where the daddy pollen comes from, the resulting seeds will grow to be plants just like the mama plant. This enables you to save seeds from year to year and get the results you are looking for.

Seed packets marked "hybrid" are a signal NOT to save seeds from the crops produced. Hybrids can often be sterile, and nothing will grow from their seeds. Seed packets that do not indicate hybrid or that say "heirloom" are usually the open-pollinated varieties that can be used to save seeds.

Thyme to Dig In

Cross-pollination affects only the *seed* produced. It won't affect the fruit and create cucchinis (cucumber + zucchini) or peppomatoes (pepper + tomatoes). If strange-looking produce is growing in your garden, it means the original plant or seed was mislabeled, not that the plants were grown too close together.

Open-pollinated doesn't guarantee the exact same produce year after year in all cases. Squash, cucumbers, and melons—to name a few—will cross with great random abandon, and the seeds will be full of surprises the next year, whether they were hybrid or not. Seeds have been saved for literally generations from these crosses; the surprises are most often little differences that may even show improvement over previous generations. The plants that are self-pollinated are most likely to consistently come true to seed.

Thyme to Dig In

Self-pollinated vegetables:
Beans, Lettuce, Chicory, Peas, Endive, Tomatoes

Insect-pollinated vegetables:
Asparagus, Broccoli, Brussels Sprouts, Cabbage, Carrots, Cauliflower, Celery, Chinese Cabbage, Cucumber, Eggplant, Kohlrabi, Melons, Onions, Parsley, Parsnips, Peppers, Pumpkin, Radishes, Rutabaga, Squash, Turnips

Thyme to Dig In

Open-pollinated tomatoes still have some variation in their fruit—one a little rounder, one will crack excessively, and some don't grow to the expected size. If you select seeds from the fruit that displays the traits you are most looking for, and do that year after year, natural selection will help you create a specific variety that is likely to become a family favorite. Remember to isolate the plants each year from any other varieties. This will help keep the pollination between just the plants you are working with.

After twenty years of selecting the best (largest, crack free, no cat facing, and so forth) tomato to save the seeds from and planting twenty or so plants the next year, one of our friends has Bart's Best! He started with a superb-tasting, ugly tomato and crossed and crossed and now has a big, superb-tasting, gorgeous tomato.

This tendency to cross can show up only in the seeds but still make a huge difference in your harvest. There are a few plants we grow exclusively to *eat* the seeds. Can you name any of them? The produce from corn, for instance, can be impacted from the first generation genetic cross because we do eat the seeds and corn is wind-pollinated. Should you plant two varieties of hybrid super sweet corn close enough for cross-pollination, the genetic code that produces super sweet corn will be compromised, and the resulting kernels will be "field corn"—that's the corn usually fed to pigs! To avoid an unexpected result from cross-pollination not of your choosing, wind-pollinated crops must be at least 1 mile from one another and separated by ¼ mile if they are insect-pollinated, according to the Colorado State University

Extension. Or choose two varieties that shed pollen weeks apart and hope your nearby neighbors aren't growing another variety of the same vegetable.

Thyme to Dig In

Self-pollinated varieties give gardeners the best chance at successful seed saving. But you can keep the bees (or other insects) from cross-pollinating the insect-pollinated varieties. Some special attention is needed if you want to assure that they will come true from their seeds. The large squash blossoms would be a good way to practice this controlled pollination. When a female blossom opens, take the male blossom and turn it inside out. Gently rub the pollen onto the center of the female blossom. Then, to ensure that the only pollen to reach the female blossom is the pollen you put there, gently close the flower and tie or band the blossom closed.

TIME TO GET GROWING

When do you start looking for seeds to plant? Certainly in early spring the racks of different seeds start appearing in home improvement stores, garden centers, and even grocery stores. Catalogs and online suppliers keep the seeds available year round. But when do you start to look for seeds from the *plants*?

BOLTING

YOUNG
RADISH

RADISH BOLTING
TO FLOWER

RADISH WITH
SEED PODS

Annual plants burst out with their flowers and the seeds by the end of their first (and only) growing season. Typical annual plants in the veggie garden include radishes, lettuce, peas, corn, and beans. When a plant ceases to grow leaves and jumps into flower production, it is said to "bolt." Once that happens, the part of the plant we usually enjoy eating becomes tough and bitter. After the flowers form, the seeds follow quickly. If you intend to save the seeds, the "fruit" must be mature and the seeds very, very dry.

BIENNIAL PLANTS

Biennial plants take two years to form flowers and then seeds. The first year the plant uses all its energy to store food. Onions, chard, and carrots are good examples of this, and we may sometimes think that this is how they were meant to spend their life. Not so. The second year, if left in the ground, flower stalks start to grow, blossom, and set seed. If the plants could talk, they would then say "ta-da!" and die. About all it takes for these biennials to produce seed the second year is to be left alone in the garden. It may be weeks until you see stems growing up from the center of the plant. These eventually will form flowers. Many of these flowers are pretty enough to go into bouquets. As the flowers begin to fade, either seeds or seedpods will begin to form. Wait until the plant dies back before harvesting the seeds.

Biennial vegetables:

Beets
Brussels Sprouts
Cabbage
Carrots
Celeriac
Celery
Collards
Kale
Kohlrabi
Leeks
Turnips
Onions
Parsley
Parsnips
Rutabaga
Swiss Chard

SWISS CHARD

Many gardeners have never seen carrot flowers because they either eat all the carrots the first year or plow the last of them under to prepare for next season's garden. Remember, if your intent is to collect seeds

CARROT UMBEL OR FLOWER

from biennial plants, you need two growing seasons. Most seed packets label if a plant is annual, biennial, or perennial.

PERENNIAL PLANTS

Perennial plants, under the right conditions, live for several years, usually producing seeds every year as soon as they mature enough to blossom. Watch for a tricky listing of some plants as perennials—it may be that they are only perennial if the area receives no killing frost during the winter. In temperate growing regions, tomatoes grow as annuals, dying as the winter cold descends. In the tropics, tomatoes grow as perennials, resulting in quite large plants. Another example is rosemary, which is often listed as a perennial. As discussed previously, Arp is the only variety that is reliable when grown outside in Zone 5. (Zone 5 has winters that consistently drop to 5–15 degrees Fahrenheit.)

After learning when the flowers will produce seeds, you can plan to harvest the seed. The fruit needs to be mature before harvesting the seeds. Seeds won't mature once the fruit is picked. Zucchini must be larger than optimum size for eating; the pods of beans must have thoroughly dried out; peppers must be starting to shrivel on the plant and probably turn a bright red or orange color.

Seeds must be thoroughly dried before storing. Any moisture allows fungi and bacteria to start growing,

and the seeds will rot. Beans should be so dry that hitting them with a hammer will cause them to shatter. Tomato seeds should crack if you try to bend them. Store the seeds in a dry location, a place that will continue to keep them very dry.

Adding a little package of desiccant to your storage container will help assure the seeds stay dry during storage. A desiccant is a material that traps any moisture that might be in the air in the container. You can buy the material, like silica gel, at a hobby store.

A cool, dark location extends the "shelf life" of stored seeds. A basement might be ideal if it isn't overly moist. A canning jar with a lid can keep most moisture out. Each individual variety of seed placed in the bottle should be in a separate little envelope. You can also store commercially packaged hybrid seeds in this way. Storing hybrid seed packets make growing these veggies possible every year, even if you can't buy the

Thyme to Dig In

The definition of *fruit* includes all parts of a plant involved with seeds—Hubbard squash, peppers, cucumbers, eggplants, and tomatoes all produce fruit even though we call them vegetables. With carrots and beets, we eat the root, not the fruit. But they are still all veggies to us!

Thyme to Dig In

How to Harvest, Clean, and Store Tomato Seeds

Choose the very best tomato when you want to harvest seeds. If you are going for the biggest tomato, choose that one as your seed source. Perhaps you want the tomato that resists cracking on the top, so select the tomato that best shows that trait. Let the tomato ripen completely—either on the vine or in the house.

Squeeze the ripe tomato over a bowl and collect the juice and seeds as they drip into the bowl. Cutting an "x" in the bottom of the tomato encourages the seeds to go into the bowl when you squeeze. Put the seeds in a quart jar and add a cup or two of water.

Place the jar outside for a few days until the seeds

start to ferment—they will look moldy, and fuzzy, and the water will be a nasty-looking color. This is not a problem; it is a solution. It is necessary to remove the jelly-like coating around the seeds before storing.

Once the stuff in the bottle looks quite disgusting, pour the mess into a fine sieve. Rinse many times until the gunk is gone and the seeds look clean. The next step is to dry the tomato seeds.

Spread the seeds on wax paper or parchment paper. If you put them on a napkin or paper towel they will stick. Stir occasionally as they dry. This may take a few days if you live in an area with little humidity. In humid areas, you may want to dry the seeds on a screen to make sure they dry completely and don't start to go moldy.

Thyme to Dig In

You can make your own desiccant. For your home-made version, buy a new box of powdered milk. (Any open box already contains moisture removed from room air.) Place 1–2 tablespoons of dry milk in the middle of a 4-inch square piece of paper towel or tissue. Fold up the sides to create a little packet and put an elastic band around the packet to secure the powdered milk. Each quart jar requires one homemade packet.

Thyme to Dig In

Germination Test

Count out 5 or 10 seeds. (Choose any number of seeds—these numbers just make it easier to figure the percentage of germination.) Place the seeds between layers of a moist paper towel. The paper towel and seeds should then be placed in something like a plastic baggie. You don't want the paper towel to dry out, so just fold over the end of the baggie. Put the baggie someplace warm and check the seeds every day. Once the first few seeds grow roots a half inch or so long, count how many actually started to grow. (2 out of 5 = 40% germination; 7 out of 10= 70% germination, and so on.)

May the seeds you sow be much more than those you put in the ground.
—Anonymous

seeds in a local store. A good practice is to always keep a year's supply of seeds on hand.

Make sure the seeds are very, very dry if you decide to store seeds in the fridge or freezer. The low temperatures will cause any moisture to condense in the fridge, and that can lead to mold. Modern frost-free freezers keep things very dry in the freezer, but little ice crystals can form if the container has any moisture in it. Be sure to use some kind of desiccant in the containers.

Seed packets marked for the current year germinate to a predetermined percentage. If you plant ten seeds, nine of them should begin to grow. After the year of packaging, the germination rate slowly declines. Some varieties decline faster than others. Sweet corn, onions, parsley, and parsnips drop in percentage quite quickly. We've planted some radish seeds more than fifteen years past date and they grew wildly to an 85 percent rate. On the other hand, a box of beans dropped to 50 percent in just two years. If necessary, you can just plant more old seeds to cover the bet or perform a germination test on the seeds in question.

LET THE PLANTING BEGIN

Planting seeds into a rich garden bed at the right time should give you the results you are looking for. Of course, there are other necessities needed for the seeds to do well. The soil must be the right temperature, and there must be sufficient moisture for the little seeds to absorb water and push out of their seed coats. Then, continue watering to keep the roots and leaves growing. Natural precipitation—in many parts of the country other than the Intermountain West, so we are told—will provide the water. Pay attention to the soil; you may need to give additional water, at least until the seedlings have grown for a while. Learn when to expect the seedlings to push their heads through the soil—don't give up on the slow growers. For example, carrots take from 14 to 21 days to sprout while radishes show up in just 3–5 days. Keep on watering and have faith in the germination process that is happening below the soil.

Seeds, soil, and water are the first three elements for seed growing. The next element, sunshine, should be appropriate to the kind of plant you are growing. Some seeds need light to germinate; others don't and should be planted more deeply. A general rule is to plant twice as deep as the seed is long. Once the little plant starts to grow, both intensity and duration of direct sunshine should be correct for the plant. Cool season crops need the angled sunshine of early spring and late fall, or you'll need to be in charge of giving them some shade. Warm season crops need full day direct sunshine.

Sunshine can directly affect the next requirement needed for seed growing: the temperature of the air and soil. The temperatures must be either cool or warm enough to allow germination. Once the seedlings are up and growing, the temperatures must stay in the correct range for good production.

Sunshine will warm the air, but moist soil may stay too cool for planting early in the season. Some crops, like peas and lettuce, require cool growing conditions. Others will tolerate cool soil, but the air should stay in the moderate range and not freezing. Carrots and beets fall into this category.

The early warm season crops need warm soil and moderate air temperatures. Tomatoes fit in this category. Late warm season crops demand very warm soil and warm air temperatures. Peppers and melons require these conditions to do well.

Soil Temperatures for Seed Germination		
Cool Season Crops	Soil temperature 40–85	Broccoli, cabbage, chard, kohlrabi, lettuce, peas, radish, spinach, and turnips
Moderate Season Crops	Soil temperature 50–85	Beets, carrots, cauliflower, lettuce, onion, parsley, parsnips, potatoes, Swiss chard
Early Warm Season Crops	Soil temperature 60–95	Beans, celery, corn, cucumbers, New Zealand spinach, and summer squash
Late Warm Season Crops	Soil temperature 70–95	Lima beans, cantaloupe, eggplant, pepper, pumpkin, winter squash, tomato, and watermelon

Air Temperatures for Best Growth	
Cool Season	60–65 degrees
Moderate	55–85 degrees
Early and Late Warm	70–90 degrees

In the Intermountain area, these temperatures can be roughly translated as these dates:

- **Cool Season:** As soon as you can work the soil, usually March 15–May 1

- **Moderate:** A week or two after Cool Season, around March 22–May 1

- **Early Warm:** Average date of last frost (mid May-ish), around the time apple trees start to bloom

- **Late Warm:** When the soil is warm, usually about 2 weeks after the early warm crops

If you ignore the requirements needed by a plant, poor results will follow. If you plant radishes in warm conditions, they quickly bolt. Peas trying to ripen in the heat turn to woody little marbles. Beans rot in cold soil—ditto with corn seeds. Melons demand very warm soil or they will sulk and not grow much at all.

Thyme to Dig In

Modifying the air and soil temperature isn't all that hard. Putting shade cloth or a garden blanket above the lettuce and spinach will prolong the harvest. Walls o' Water temper both soil and air. Clear plastic laid on the soil for a week before planting warms the soil nicely. Using warm water to fill the hole before planting the warm season crops gives an extra measure of comfort to the roots. (For more information, see the conclusion.)

WHY BOTHER GROWING YOUR OWN SEEDLINGS?

After pricing the transplants (small plants ready to grow in your garden), it isn't a stretch to think you can save money if you buy the seeds and start them yourself. After all, it's three dollars for three plants vs. two dollars for fifty seeds. However, as a friend once said, "If it were all that easy for a gardener to grow her own plants from seeds, do you think these nurseries would keep doing it?" It is deceptively easy to get the seed to start growing. Growing the tiny plant long enough to become a stocky transplant ready to go into your garden is a different kettle of beans altogether.

If you've ever experienced the crushing anguish of seeing tiny green seedlings emerge and then fail to thrive and even die, you know the bewilderment when you thought you did everything right. A window, even a south-facing window, just won't do. Sure, the little seeds poke their heads up, but within days the stem is pencil-lead thin, and white in color, with puny, teensy leaves growing inches apart. Lest you think that's just the way seeds grow, consider this: the first two leaves should sit pretty much right on the soil and the next leaves, called true leaves, should be just barely above them. No, they shouldn't look like giraffe necks with a tiny green bow tie on top.

Should determination, or finances, drive you to "grow your own," a fluorescent light fixture can fill in for sunshine quite nicely. A four-foot shop light with one cool white light bulb and one warm white light bulb sufficiently mimics the wavelengths of sunshine that little seedlings need to flourish. There are also grow lights developed specifically for this purpose. Just keep the tops of the young plants within an inch or two of the light bulb. This usually means you need to raise the light as the plants grow or lower the plants as they get taller. You will need to rotate the containers from under the center of the lights to the ends and from the front to the back to make sure all seedlings get the same amount of light.

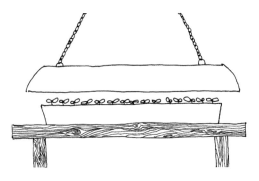

And that's why you may not want to bother trying to start seedlings on your windowsill. On the other hand, for years and years Joy's friend Jean put her little pots of seeds on the windowsill in her *unheated garage*. The window does face south, but the windowsill is only 5 inches wide and the window is only six feet long. Along with the fact that she sings to her plants, she also never tells the seedlings they can't grow there! Admittedly, the

little starts are just a bit leggy, but they flourish in her garden, always supplying a bountiful harvest.

> If you obey all the rules, you miss all the fun.
> — Katherine Hepburn

TIMING IS EVERYTHING

This homegrown adventure needs to take into consideration the best date on the calendar to plant the seeds. Advice always mentions counting back from the date of the average last frost. The logic is that by the time the seedlings have grown to transplant size, it will be safe to set them out in the garden. Here is where a little information from your local extension office makes your gardening more successful. Every county has one—just do a search online for the one nearest you. Not only will they have information about the average last frost, but they will also have information on which varieties of plants should be started when.

HARDENING OFF

A transition shock from inside to outside lays low many a sturdy transplant.

Thyme to Dig In

"Damping off" is a fungal disease that attacks seedlings, especially when started indoors, and is characterized by a sudden wilting or collapsing at the soil line. Use a fork as a rake and gently work the soil around the seedling allowing air circulation. Watering with chamomile tea may also help prevent the disease.

Inside: steady temperature	Outside: temperatures vary wildly
Inside: pleasant calm air	Outside: wind from that direction, then this direction, then that direction
Inside: gentle, soothing, consistent light	Outside: glaring blasts of direct sunshine
Inside: regular drinks of water	Outside: drought, flood, drought, flood, drought

You can moderate these wild swings in conditions with a little extra effort. A process called "hardening off" gradually eases the babies into the hard, cruel garden. Put the little ones out in a shady, protected area for a couple of hours a day for three or four days— or at least a day or two. For the next couple of days the plants should spend a half-day in the protected shade. Then, it's on to the bright light of day for a few morning hours. By now your nerve and the plants' vigor should allow for the first overnighter in the out of doors. But keep an eye on the weather forecast and monitor possible dips in overnight temperatures.

Once you've worked at getting them ready, take a deep breath and plant the starts in your garden. Be gentle when you work with their little roots. Try to keep the moist soil around the fragile roots as you slip them into the planting hole. If it is early in the season and the soil is still quite cool, pour warm water into the hole to warm the soil.

Thyme to Dig In

When you buy a young plant from the nursery, always check the roots. If they are matted and tangled, use force to separate the roots on most veggies. Roots will continue to grow in circles if you don't ruffle them. They can become stunted and never grow much at all.
Note: Melons do not appreciate this treatment.

The best of all possible planting/transplanting weather would be a moderate temperature day with cloud cover and promise of a gentle rain for the next couple of days. But it usually works out so there is a hot wind and blazing sunshine predicted.

You can take pity on your tomato-sandwich-to-be by making a little tent out of cardboard, scrap wood, or anything that can be propped up to shade the plants for the first couple of days in the garden. All little baby plants appreciate this extra care—veggies and flowers alike.

COLD FRAMES

You can use a contraption that will give seedlings the protection they need as well as provide real outside air and modified temperatures. Cold frames are easy to construct and, if you have old windows for the adjustable lid, they are not expensive. Sides can be made of old lumber, bales of straw, plywood, or nearly anything else that will support the lid. The lid needs to be transparent to both allow in the sunshine and trap the extra heat that will build up during the day. Then at night, the heat is held in when you close the lid. When you make the back of the frame taller than the front, you can angle the box to do its best imitation of a greenhouse.

Cold frames are not the same as greenhouses but do allow a gardener a specific place to harden off transplants. You can get them out and into garden soil much earlier than it would be possible if they were planted directly into the actual garden. By opening and closing the glass or plastic lid, you can keep the heat in or let the heat out as needed. Be diligent—a sunny day can raise the temperature to the point the little plants could cook! If the lid is left open on a cold night, freezing could doom your early start in the garden. A cold frame is an ideal place to harden off seedlings that you've grown inside your house. It's an equally super place to directly plant your first crop of lettuce, broccoli, and chard.

Lettuce, radishes, and little green onions for a salad in February is exactly what encourages many gardeners to make room for a little cold frame. If cool temperatures come and go in a blink in your area, keeping your lettuce in the cold frame can free up garden space for crops that don't mind summer coming nearly on the heels of winter. After the lettuce harvest, you can use the frame to do the starting and hardening off for your later warm season crops.

THE REASON TO BOTHER

A provident gardener looks to the future. And seeds are future plants. To provide fresh or preserved vegetables, it is necessary to either have someone else sell you seeds and plants or grow and save them yourself. Seeds do store well—in the *right* place under the *right* conditions. *Cool, dark,* and *dry* are the words to remember. Seeds do not do well started in little containers filled with regular garden soil. Therefore, storing potting soil, small containers, and maybe an extra light source is needed to prepare for when the choice is between starting your own transplants or having none at all.

Thyme to Dig In

Vermiculite (puffed mica rock) is a great medium to use when starting seeds. It stores longer than potting soil. Vermiculite can stay dry forever and still be used. Once potting soil dries out, it becomes difficult to get it moist again, but it is worth storing to have if and when you need to put the seedlings in a little bigger pot. When you need to rehydrate the potting soil before planting, use water that is very, very hot. Peat moss won't absorb cold water.

Growing your own plants from seeds can be as simple or elaborate as you want or as is needed. Being prepared is the key. Potting soil, cold frame, seeds, light fixture, tools—your list should be as long or short as you can manage. Start with a few attempts at growing transplants to get the hang of it. Sinking all your gardening money into something that will just give you heartburn and disappointment is never a good idea. Begin while you can still buy seeds and produce at the store as a backup. You never know when it will be too late, so now is the time to learn and practice the basics. Everything you learn brings smiles as well as good things to eat, so whether or not the pushing has become shoving, your garden will thank you with beauty and nourishment.

"When it starts raining, it is too late to begin building the ark ... we do need to listen to the Lord's spokesmen. We need to calmly continue to move ahead and to prepare for what will surely come. We need not panic or fear, for if we are prepared, spiritually and temporally, we and our families will survive any flood. Our arks will float on a sea of faith if our works have been steadily and surely preparing for the future." (W. Don Ladd, "Make Thee an Ark," *Ensign*, Nov. 1994, 28.)

FAQs

What kind of soil should I use to start my seeds?

Not your garden soil, regardless of how good you think it is. That soil contains fungus and bacteria that may cause plant diseases. Use a sterile mix or vermiculite.

What causes my seedlings to start growing and then quickly die?

Sudden death of tiny seedlings is a sign of a fungal disease called damping-off. Next time try using a sterile medium to start the seeds in. There are bags of specific mixes sold that are good for starting seeds. You can also cover the seeds with either washed sand or small grade vermiculite to keep the fungal spores from getting to the little stems.

I don't have little peat pots from the nursery. What can I use to start my seeds?

Nearly any container that holds potting mix and allows drainage can be used: egg cartons, yogurt containers with holes in the bottom, small nursery pots, or half egg shells with a small hole in the bottom (then gently crack the shell just before planting out in the garden.)

How many seeds should I plant in a hill?

In gardening talk, a hill is not a small mountain. It is a group of seeds, sometimes planted in a small mound of soil maybe 2 or 3 inches tall. Usually four or five seeds are planted in the group, and then the seedlings are thinned down to the strongest two plants by clipping the others off at the ground. Don't pull them—pulling ruffles the roots of the remaining seedlings.

Where can I get seeds for really unusual plants?

Besides the terrific catalogs that can come in the mail, the wonder of the Internet immediately opens the world of strange and unusual plants. Try Richters.com for herbs; Baker Creek at rareseeds.com for heirloom varieties of vegetables; Cooksgarden.com and NicholsGardenNursery.com for international varieties; and TotallyTomato.com for—go ahead, guess—tomatoes!

How far apart should I plant my pea seeds?

Pea seeds can be planted as close as an inch apart. A row four inches wide will give better production than a single row of seeds. Scattering the peas an inch apart in the wide row increases by at least three times the number of pea plants per foot of row.

How warm does it need to be before I plant my seeds outside?

The soil temperature is what counts. Check to see if you are dealing with cool season or warm season plants. Some veggies can go out as soon as you can work the soil—others must have warm (at least 60 degrees) soil to germinate and grow well.

Why do my plants turn white when I plant them out in the garden?

Plants can get sunburned when first exposed to direct sunlight. Unlike gardeners, plants don't turn red; they turn white when sunburned. Coming from a nursery doesn't mean a little plant has been out in the direct sun. Nurseries often keep their plants under a shade cloth cover to reduce the need to water as often. And any plants started in your house aren't ready to jump right out in the sun. Move plants from inside to outside gradually. Time the move on a shady day if possible. Planting in the evening will give a little time to recover, but the plants may still need some protection during the sunny part of the day for a while.

What is a Jiffy 7?

It is a clever little hockey puck–looking disk made from compressed peat moss covered with a very fine plastic netting. When the Jiffy 7 is placed in warm water, the peat absorbs the water and begins to swell. The final product is about 2 inches tall and 1½ across. On one end, the mesh has a small opening where you push a seed into the hole. You plant the entire little container in the ground when it is time for the plant to go outside.

How do you make a seed tape?

A seed tape is a way to pre-space seeds before they are planted. Commercial seed tapes are quite expensive, but you can create a homemade version. Toilet paper or one-ply paper towels work well. Cut the paper into two-inch wide strips. Mix a little flour with water to create a thin "paste." Using a toothpick, put a dot of the paste about halfway in on one edge of the paper. Space the dots of paste according to how far apart the seeds should be planted. Put two or three seeds on each dot, and then fold over the paper, creating a long tape with seeds running down the middle. Allow the paste to dry before planting. Create the usual furrow for seeds and then lay the seed tape in the bottom of the furrow, cover with soil, and water well.

Chapter 4: Quick, Pull Up the Drawbridge!

Now and then, a gardener experiences a few disappointments and frustrations. One such scenario is to discover that the temperature dropped below freezing during the night, and the once vibrant green and healthy plants are now wilted and black. Or it may be the realization that a critter or two (or more) feasted on your prize-sized cabbage when you weren't looking. With a little preparation and forethought, a provident gardener can avoid or overcome these destructive annoyances by providing protection against the critters and the elements.

TEMPERING THE TEMPERATURE

In terms of temperature and sunshine, gardeners often create the very problems they are trying to solve. Everyone knows temperatures that weaken or kill plants are determined by elements, like the quirky weather, latitude, and altitude in and around your garden. But it was you, dear gardener, who chose the plants being planted outside. And you were in charge of deciding which location they would occupy in the garden.

Plants have a range of temperatures in which they grow well. At the cold end is the temperature below which they will just plain die. There is also a cool temperature that is about the lowest in which they can still barely grow. Optimum range is where they would always grow if they had their druthers. And finally, there is the high temperature above which the plant can't sustain growth.

The cold end of the thermometer seems to wave a red flag in front of the bull. Gardeners love to push, push, push, and test the limit of the zone listed for a plant. The USDA determines zone listings. These help gardeners estimate whether their zone is appropriate for a plant they like. Low zone numbers indicate winters with harsh below-zero conditions. As the numbers increase, the winter temperatures get warmer. Zone 2 is the harshest zone a gardener can face realistically. Zones 3 and 4 are often found in our higher mountain valleys. Lower valley areas along the Wasatch Front are classified as Zone 5a or 5b. By the time you get to the southern end of Utah, gardens are enjoying Zone 8 or 9. (See Zone Chart in appendix.)

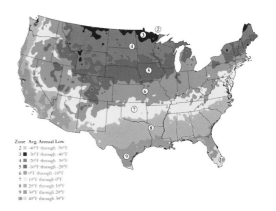

Zone	Avg. Annual Low
2	-40°F through -50°F
3	-30°F through -40°F
4	-20°F through -30°F
5	-10°F through -20°F
6	0°F through -10°F
7	10°F through 0°F
8	20°F through 10°F
9	30°F through 20°F
10	40°F through 30°F

Undaunted by the Zone designation of their own gardens, Zone 5 gardeners regularly flaunt the Zone 6 and 7 tags and gleefully cart their plants home. Sometimes a neighbor who has that particular plant (growing just fine, thank you) in their garden spurs on this confidence. What most of us don't know is the effort it takes to create the conditions that allow that admired plant to thrive.

A small area that does not keep to the list of zonal conditions is called a "micro-climate." Creating such a place in your garden is a technically challenging effort—not usually the project a novice or moderately experienced gardener would like to tackle. Is it possible in almost any garden? Yes. Does it take considerable research? Yes. Unless you have connections with a gardener who already knows just how to do this, we recommend you choose plants that will have fewer challenges in your garden. Zone 5 people, plant Zone 5 plants. Zone 4 gardeners, plant Zone 4 plants. If you must be daring, slide up only one zone number, and good luck. Beware: attempting to go up a zone may work for a year or two, but eventually conditions will strike down that prized plant.

Even in appropriate zones, garden plants face serious temperature attacks: an extra cool spring, a surprisingly hot summer, a fall that lasts about sixteen hours, snow that doesn't melt until Mother's Day, or an unexpected cold front blasting down from the Arctic. All these can throw temperature expectations right out the window. Plants need to be protected from the cool or cold temperatures in the spring and fall. A record-low winter temperature may come once a decade, but that just may happen this next year. Forewarned should be forearmed. At the other end of the thermometer, summer temperatures may exceed the limits of a garden plant's growing range and need to be moderated.

SPRING PROTECTION

In areas where spring gradually emerges from winter's white grasp and progresses calmly toward sunny summer, protection isn't usually a topic of conversation or concern. But in the parts of the country where spring is more like a Slinky, sliding back and forth, and up and down, protection is on the mind of all gardeners. The gardeners with the most to lose are those who tried to get their tender plants in the ground during the first glimpse of spring. Other gardeners with a more pragmatic view are content to wait to see how many times the neighbor's tomatoes freeze before deciding to put plants outside in their own garden. The size of your garden determines how much you can reasonably protect. Obviously, a smaller area is easier to protect than a larger space.

But even conservative gardeners can be caught with their Hot Caps down. Weather changes so quickly that the late weather reports completely miss the fast-moving cold front, and, oops, there goes another row of tomato plants. It will help if you at least have a few of the materials needed to protect individual or groups of plants.

Because cold air is heavier than warm air, it sinks. Temperatures are always coldest near the ground and in low areas. "Breaking the frost" simply means putting something between the plants and the sinking cold air. Almost anything can be used to break a light frost. But there is a difference between a light frost and a heavy freeze. Nearly anything over a plant will protect it between 33 and 30 degrees. If temperatures drop below 25 degrees, it may take more than a thin layer of protection to do any good for your plants. An additional source of heat, like a string of Christmas lights (non-LED), a trouble light, and so forth may need to be added under some sort of cover.

In chapter 3 there is information about making a cold frame. Cold frames can offer some protection from light frosts as long as you remember to close the lid at night. And if it is a warm, sunny day, remember to vent the lid so the temperature doesn't rise so high that it kills the plants you just saved from a frosty death.

Thyme to Dig In

Constructing hoop houses over a raised bed garden box or even over a long, single row is easy and quick to put together.

In the four corners of a square box, pound an 18-inch piece of rebar halfway into the ground either inside or outside the box. Slip ½-inch PVC pipe over the rebar, crossing over to the opposite side. Secure the two pieces together where they meet at the top with some sturdy string, wire, or a zip tie. This creates a frame that can be used in a variety of ways. When covered with clear plastic, it makes a mini greenhouse to protect plants from too cool or cold weather. (When the sun is shining, lift the sides for adequate ventilation or it will get too hot inside. Put the sides down for the night.) If more protection is needed, throw an old sleeping bag on top for more insulation. For rectangular boxes or for a row garden, place the rebar and PVC pipe covered-wagon style, spaced about 3–4 feet apart.

When hot weather comes, shade cloth can be substituted to keep plants cool as needed.

If pests are a problem, insect netting over the frame will keep them out.

Going a step further, chicken wire could even be placed over the frame to keep out the bigger critters. This works well on a square frame constructed from PVC in "tinker-toy" fashion.

Thyme to Dig In

By adding Christmas lights inside a cover over plants, the temperature will increase enough to protect from freezing.

Thyme to Dig In

Walls O' Water* are beneficial to extend the growing season for warm-weather vegetables such as tomatoes and peppers. This cylinder with channels of water is slipped over the plants. The water absorbs heat from the sun during the day and releases it back to the plant during the cooler night. Walls O' Water protect not only against freezing temperatures but also from chilling temperatures that dip into the 40s and 50s. Tomatoes flourish in moderate 65–85-degree temperatures. When night temperatures are consistently above 55 degrees, the Walls O' Water can be removed. The Walls O' Water help hold water in the soil so take care not to overwater the plants.

Before placing a Wall O' Water around a plant, first turn a 5-gallon bucket upside down around the plant. Place the Wall O' Water on the outside of the bucket, fill with water, then reach down and pull out the bucket. This leaves the Wall O' Water firmly surrounding the plant.

On extra cold nights, a plastic garbage bag can be placed upside down over the wall to provide additional protection—almost like a mini greenhouse. Be sure and poke a few holes in the garbage bag to allow any rain water to drain through.

*This device is known by a variety of names: Water Walls, Walls of Water, Insulating Teepee, Kozy Coat. Depending on the brand, they come in green, white, or red. By whatever name they're known, they serve the same purpose!

Thyme to Dig In

When an unexpected light frost is in the forecast and tender plants are in the ground, simply push some slightly taller stakes into the soil for support and cover the area with whatever you have on hand. It may look for a while like the laundry basket has been emptied in the yard, but extra bed sheets and blankets can protect in a pinch.

Other Frost Stoppers:
Cold frame
Hot Cap
Cardboard box
Bottomless milk jug
Tunnel row cover
Bucket

SUMMER PROTECTION

Shady areas in the garden can offer some relief from the summer heat. Gardeners should take this into consideration when deciding where to plant their cool season veggies. You can tuck lettuce, spinach, or radishes in shade to partial shade areas where warm season veggies couldn't do well. Gardener-made shade can also offer relief as the temperature climbs. A frame made from just about anything the gardener has handy will support a light frost blanket as well as a section of shade cloth. Shade cloth is a woven material that is manufactured to allow only a percentage of the sunlight through. You can find 50, 60, or 70 percent shade cloth at most full-service garden centers and nurseries.

> ### Thyme to Dig In
>
> **Shade:** At most 2–3 hours of direct sun; filtered sun for most of the day
>
> **Partial Shade/Sun:** 3–6 hours of direct sun
>
> **Full Sun:** 8 hours or more of direct sunshine
>
> Note: Plants that tolerate full sun in lower altitudes or southern states may need partial shade in high altitudes and northern areas.

Gardeners can plan ahead for plant-supplied shade. Tender edibles, both flowers and veggies, can be planted on the north side of crops, shrubs, or trees. Whether they are raspberries or corn, the taller plants will shade the shorter crops. Shade won't help much when the air temperature hovers around 100 degrees, but the cool season plants will stay productive longer in the shade of their garden companions.

FALL PROTECTION

Days get shorter and sunlight becomes less intense as the fall season approaches, and gardeners start listening for the first forecasts of possible frost. The same protection used in springtime can be put to use again. The one difference this time around is that the temperatures will continue, perhaps erratically, to get steadily cooler and won't warm again until the next growing season.

Some plants can be protected from frost, but the reprieve may do very little good. If the days are too short to allow tomatoes, peppers, and other warm season crops to ripen, gardeners might just as well let the frost put them out of their misery. Winter squash can tolerate a light frost and can be left in the field. But the softer crops should be picked and taken in the house.

WINTER PROTECTION

Snow is an excellent insulator. With consistent snow cover, plants are not exposed to drastically cold temperatures. By late winter, the snow remaining on the ground can keep the garden soil from drying out and warming up. During sunny days, a sheet of clear plastic over the snow can trap the heat and speed up the melting.

SOUTHWEST WINTER DAMAGE

Trees with thin bark are susceptible to damage during winter months. Young fruit trees have thin bark and need protection. Either white tree wrap or white latex paint can be used. The idea is to keep the bark cool. When warmer winter temperatures combine with direct sunshine on the south and west side of a tree trunk, temperatures can go well above freezing just under the bark.

This is no problem during the daytime, but when night comes and temperatures fall well below freezing, the fluid freezes. Now that's a problem! Cells are killed when the freezing liquid swells and breaks the cell walls. This damage isn't visible right away. But when the growing season begins, cracks show up running up and down the trunk. Bark will peel, exposing wood and the living tissue. The wound in the bark allows disease organisms and insects to invade the tree. Even without those invaders, it causes a long scar to develop on the trunk.

OVERWINTERING INSIDE

Tender plants like lemon and orange trees can be grown even in colder climates. Of course, you can't just wave at them from the warmth of your house while they're shivering in the snowy weather. In the high altitude of Park City, Utah, an orange tree has been known to supply fragrant blossoms, little green oranges, and ripe oranges at the same time! The little tree was brought back from California in the 1930s. It was potted into an old wringer washing machine and wheeled from the little front  room to the back porch to the backyard and back inside every year for over sixty years. When Joy's great-grandmother died, the tree was given as a gift to Park City and lived many more years, first in the front window of the Utah Power and Light office and later in the town library.

WIND PROTECTION

Ferocious winds can topple tall trees and whip branches from every bush around. But even steady or occasional gusty winds can also do damage in the garden. Young plants are at risk of losing too much water. When wind blows across leaves, more water is lost due to transpiration. The young plants have not had time to establish many roots to take up sufficient replacement water. The poor little plants may wilt right down from water loss caused by the breezes. A tunnel row cover or Hot Cap may provide protection until the transplants get established. Some transplants are skinny and tall, so even lots of roots won't keep the stems from being broken by a few good gusts of wind.

Wind affects the soil and its ability to hold water for the plants. Limited water supply requires that the water delivered be available to the roots of the plants. The unprotected surface of garden soil allows a good deal of water to evaporate before it reaches the roots. Hot and windy weather will create the greatest loss, but even if the temperature is moderate, the wind will still do the deed.

Mulch of nearly every kind will reduce the water loss. Mulch can also protect and nourish the soil.

Thyme to Dig In

Mulch can offer protection when placed on top of the garden soil. It is mainly used to hold the moisture in and keep the weeds out. It also keeps the soil at a fairly even temperature. A thick layer of organic mulch in the fall over tender plants can protect against hard winters.

Organic mulches:

Bark (shredded)
Compost
Grass clippings (in moderation)
Leaves (shredded)
Newspapers—thick layer watered down. Invisible when topped with compost or another mulch
Hay or straw—may introduce weed seed
Wood chips

Inorganic mulches:

Pea gravel—used in xeric gardens
Black plastic—holds moisture, deters weeds, keeps fruit clean
Red plastic—said to increase tomato yields

Thyme to Dig In

Provide a windbreak for tender plants by driving poles into the ground around a section of garden or the corners of a raised box. Attach some shade cloth or other fabric to the poles, leaving the top open. The wind is subdued and the sun still shines inside.

Organic mulches like bark, manures, and compost gradually decompose and release nutrients needed by the plants. For water conservation, any type of mulch can be effective, but to benefit the soil, the mulch should have an organic origin.

PROTECTING TREE TRUNKS

Newly planted fruit or nut trees, as well as shade and ornamental varieties, are vulnerable to steady or gusty winds. Steady winds slowly, almost imperceptibly, cause the trees to grow at an angle. Drive through a neighborhood at the mouth of any canyon and you can see the results of this tilt. To compensate a little for this gentle push in one direction, plant the tree with the trunk at about a 10–15-degree slant into

Thyme to Dig In

Gusty winds, often from different directions, can pose a problem. Since the young tree has not established roots into the existing soil, the only anchor it has is its root ball. Little trunks with even smaller branches aren't always bothered, even when the trunk may be ten feet tall. When the leaves are present, however, the treetop becomes a sail, catching every puff of wind that blows by. Because the pressure isn't steady, the tree begins to rock back and forth, literally moving whichever way the wind blows.

If you anticipate this problem, staking becomes an easy protection you can give to these young trees. Staking should not be done as a routine part of planting a tree. The tree grows stronger wood if the trunk is allowed to move a little bit in the wind. The staking described here is for the trees that would otherwise end up parallel with the ground instead of perpendicular.

A single pole may be used to secure the tree.* Position the pole at the time the tree is put in the ground. That assures that the roots won't be damaged when the post is driven in. The binding material used should be soft with a little give, or stretch, in it. A wire will most certainly cut into the bark of the tree, damaging or even killing it. Rather than making a loop around the trunk and post, like an oval hula-hoop, make a figure 8. The tree is in one circle of the eight, the post in the other. This gives some leeway for the tree to move a little and protects the bark from being scraped. The post should be on the side of the tree that is windward (the direction the wind comes from most often), if possible.

*There are also the 2- or 3-post and the 2- or 3-tent stake methods of supporting a tree. (Refer to *Joy in Your Garden*, pp. 38–40.)

the wind. It looks a little odd when the tree is young, but the result in ten years or so is a tree that is more closely upright than others in the vicinity.

CRITTERS OVER WHICH WE MAY HAVE SOME CONTROL

Because we try to use and recommend the least toxic controls possible, some of the most advertised and promoted chemicals will not be discussed in this chapter. It isn't difficult for a gardener to find that information. You will find many who are glad to indoctrinate, er, we mean *teach* you about the possibilities of using poisonous chemicals in your garden and around your home. But we won't be among them.

"Provident control" may be defined as trying to avoid the problems in the first place. Think ahead before you choose plants to grow in your garden. If you want to plant "snail candy"—like peas, beans, or spinach—prepare the area around your beds to be a less hospitable hiding place for slimy slugs and snails. These voracious plant eaters need some place to hide during sunny days. They prefer to be under

almost anything (slugs) and beneath low-growing plants (snails). Clear a no-mollusk-zone for many feet around the garden, any garden, whether it is integrated, ornamental, or edible.

The bare-ground zone approach gives you space to patrol for the intruders. A flashlight and a bucket become weapons of meager destruction. Visit your garden very early in the morning and after it is dark at night. Remember, for every slug or snail you plop into the bucket you have just prevented another one, two, or three hundred babies from joining the ranks of plant eaters. *Every* slug and snail is capable of laying eggs; every one is a potential "mama."

This bare space gives you room to put down some kind of barrier. Finely ground eggshells, diatomaceous earth, or a light dusting of wood ashes will slow the slugs and snails down. You do need to reapply after every rain or snowstorm. When you use overhead sprinklers as your irrigation method, putting down dry material (in order for it to be effective) becomes quite time-consumingly tedious and very expensive. Drip irrigation in just the growing areas, though, will keep the paths and no-mollusk zone dry and perfect for some kind of deterrent.

Thyme to Dig In

You could use the AB board method to eliminate the snails. Place the snails on board A and then drop board B on top of board A. Well . . . you get the picture.

Both slugs and snails leave a silvery trail of slime wherever they go. You can tell if you have one or the other, or both, by looking closely at that trail. They have rasping mouthparts and will eat nearly any tender green material they find. That means new growth is particularly at risk. Floating row cover, properly secured, will keep the slimesters off the plants until the young and new plants toughen up a bit. Some plants are really snail and slug treats even when they are full-grown. For instance, if you plant hosta, they will come. You have been warned.

Thyme to Dig In

A snail leaves a dotted trail; a continuous trail indicates a slug has slid past.

INSECTS

Most insects are actually beneficial in the garden. Either they pollinate crops to ensure fruit production or they are busy eating some more injurious relative. Rest assured, any chemical insecticide is far more deadly to the good guys than to the bad guys. And just because you do spot a "bug" munching or sucking the juice out of your plant, that doesn't mean the damage will be enough to raise the warning flag.

If you want beneficial insects to be your bug-eating patrol, there must be some bugs left for them to eat!

Thyme to Dig In

What is a bug? We call nearly all creepy-crawly critters in the garden *bugs*. But a true bug is a six-legged insect with sucking mouthparts. If a chunk was eaten from your plant, a bug didn't do it! A slug, grasshopper, or Cutter bee maybe, but not a true bug.

Leave a few weeds around areas of the garden, and they will become a hideout for the bugs that will be food to others. If weeds don't appeal to your neat garden tendencies, just steel yourself and let some of your intentional plants be nibbled a little.

Insects do most of their damage by either sucking plant juices or munching on the plants. It helps narrow down the suspects if you determine which kind of damage has been done in the garden. Some sucking insects, like aphids, show up in horrendous numbers but still do little damage to the plants. A good hard squirt of water every few days can be a very effective control. Or just benign neglect will allow time for the Lady Bug cavalry to ride, or fly, to the rescue. Learn to recognize the good guys so you can shower them with praise when they come to eat some of the destructive insects in your garden.

ADULT LADYBUG

LADYBUG LARVA

Protecting your garden plants may mean placing a barrier between the plant and the offending insect, as follows:

Cutworm: Collar around young stem made from a can, TP cardboard roll, yogurt container with bottom removed, or so forth.

Codling moth: Adult: apply sticky gooey stuff on trunk of tree.

Larvae (worm): spray kaolin clay on young apples.

Cabbage Loopers: Floating row cover.

Earwigs: If you can't keep the insect from the plant, maybe you can lure it to a quick demise. Earwigs go anyplace where they can squeeze between two surfaces. They need to feel a surface on both their back and belly at the same time. These places include under anything left out on the ground, between halves of apricots, and between rose petals. Using this knowledge, you can set traps that reduce their numbers considerably.

The Newspaper Trap: Roll a section of newspaper loosely and dip it in water to moisten the pages. Set the newspaper near the edge of your garden in the evening. Early in the morning pick up the paper (aka earwig hotel), put it in a plastic bag, secure the end, and drop the trap in the garbage.

The Grapefruit Lure: After enjoying your half grapefruit, invert the rind and put a small wadded up piece of paper under the dome of the grapefruit. Early in the morning, scoop up the paper using the grapefruit, dump the paper in a secured plastic bag, and then toss in the garbage. Pick the trap up, dust the trap off, and start all over again . . . humming the song if it seems appropriate.

LARGER MAMMAL PESTS

From little six-legged insects to much larger, four-footed plant munchers, it seems like they all want the same thing you do: healthy fresh veggies and fruit for breakfast, lunch, dinner, and occasional snacks.

Deer

The story of deer in the garden is one of invasion and theft of property. The accusers? Deer. The defendants? Gardeners. Perhaps gardeners would claim to be  the injured party, but according to the deer, people have been usurping their habitat for decades. Then, to compound the problem, people plant the most tasty plants a deer has ever tasted. What is a deer to do? They just want the best for themselves and their families!

Okay, it's a matter of perspective. From the gardener's point of view, deer are varmints that need to be removed from the premises—preferably permanently. But that just isn't likely to happen. Therefore a not-so-peaceful coexistence is called for.

Several products—commercial and homemade— are supposed to keep deer from eating garden plants  when sprayed on foliage. But if the deer are hungry enough, they will eat almost any plant they can reach. Basically, it is up to the gardener to keep the deer out of the garden. If not out of the garden, at least keep the deer from reaching the plants!

Fences are the only fairly sure-fire remedy. And very tall fences at that—8 feet tall. Or perhaps two 4-foot tall fences that are about 3–4 feet apart. A loud dog works, but neighbors may not be pleased. A motion-activated sprinkler can have some effect—and startle the cats that wander by as well. Some gardeners have built chicken wire cages for their garden plants. And wrapped trunks with chicken wire. And wrapped evergreens with burlap. And sometimes these things work too.

Gophers and Other Burrowing Animals

Once you decide against poison or traps, a barrier becomes the protection most likely to save your garden plants. If you are saying, "Whoa! I want to poison or trap the pesky burrowing beasts," then head to your local hardware store, and beasties beware. For the kinder, gentler way, we recommend hardware cloth. This is a metal mesh, with ¼- to ½-inch holes, made from heavy gauge wire.

You can line a single planting hole or a row or an entire raised bed. Using heavy duty wire cutters or a special blade on a circular saw, cut a piece of the "cloth" the size of the hole, or bed, plus 12–18 inches additional width and length. Cut and bend the cloth to create a "pan" with sides 6–8 inches deep. The hardware cloth can also be stapled right to the bottom of a raised box before flipping it over.

Fill the planting area or raised bed with good soil. From just looking at the area, you'll never know there is a gopher-stopper under your garden. This contraption is effective in protecting only the underground portion of your plants, but it does eliminate the cartoon-like disappearance of veggies being literally pulled underground by the rodents.

TO SUM IT UP

A little extra effort goes a long way in defending your crops against marauding invaders—be it weather or critters. Learn from your neighbors, garden clubs, extension offices, books, and experience. For every perfect solution, there is a problem that will be the exception. Of course, that particular problem may not ever show up again; or next time the solution may even make the problem worse. Don't despair—there is always *next* year in the garden.

FAQs

How do I kill ALL the bugs in my garden?
Whoa there, gardening friend! From one perspective that may seem like an understandable question, but there are far more beneficial insects, spiders, and other creepy things in the garden than there are harmful ones. Both for the larger environment and your own personal gardening space, you should allow nature to do most of the bug control. Good guys eat bad guys, bad guys feed good guys—balance. If there are more bad guys than the good guys can handle, either just wait a bit or hit the bad guys with a firm spray of water. Intervention with chemical warfare on your part is more likely to kill off your allies than put a dent in the number of enemies. Studies show that beneficial insects are very susceptible to insecticides. You can go after specific problems after you have identified what bad guy is causing the problem. For instance, it is a waste of time, money, energy, and product to spray for grasshoppers if it is snails doing the damage. And that doesn't even cover the terrible amount of poison released into your living and gardening environment.

Does human hair really keep deer out of gardens?
Some deer, maybe, don't like the smell. Try asking your local hairdresser or barbershop if you can stop by and collect a bag of hair. And the dirtier the hair, the better it seems to work. Make a few bags out of thin cheesecloth or netting, fill the bags with the cut hair, and hang them around the perimeter of your property. Hang a few extra over your favored plants. Keep the height of the bag about where the deer's nose would be.

What about hanging soap from fruit trees to keep away the deer?
It appears that Irish Spring or Lifebuoy are among the scents that deter some deer. Hang bars of the soap in the same kind of bags made for using human hair. Slice the soap in a few pieces—it releases more scent that way.

Are snails good for anything?
They are thought to be especially tasty with butter and garlic. However, in the garden the only time they are of some good is if you have ducks and geese—they love to eat slugs and snails.

What do box elder bugs eat? Do they bite people?
Adult box elder bugs munch on seeds found on the ground and some foliage. There is not enough damage to plants to be noticeable. Box elder bugs cannot bite people. If they are stepped on, they leave a stain that resembles brownish blood, but it is just bug innards.

How do you know if a plant has spider mites?
The first symptom is often a change in the leaf color. Leaves may appear mottled, dusty, or sort of grayish. Growth will slow way down and the plant may lose some leaves. Green beans are particularly prone to red spider mites. Sometimes you can see the teeny mites on the underside of the leaves. If the infestation is bad, you may also spot their really little webs.

If you can't see the actual mites, try taking a white envelope and putting it under some of the leaves. Flick the leaves with your fingers and check what falls on the white paper. Look really closely at the dust, and if it is moving around, the plant probably has mites. Run your finger over the moving dust. If there is a rusty red streak, then they are red spider mites and need to be controlled. Spray every three days for nine days with a natural garlic-pepper spray or with a citrus oil spray; these should eliminate the problem. The healthier the plant, the less likely a spider mite infestation will occur.

Are spiders eating my plants?

Absolutely not. Even though you see many, many webs, spiders only eat critters, not plants. The more "bugs" in the garden, the more webs and spiders will be present.

Should you pour gasoline on weeds to kill them?

No. Petroleum products kill plants but they also contaminate the soil for a very long time and can move down through the soil profile and pollute the ground water.

How do I know what zone my garden is in?

You can check the current USDA (United States Department of Agriculture) map, or ask a nursery professional at a garden center near you what zone you live in. The local county extension office will also be able to give you that information.

Will a lemon tree live outside all year in Zone 4?

Oh no! But it can enjoy your couple of summer months outside and then be moved indoors to live with you during the long cold season. For saving its life, it will probably reward you with fragrant lemon flowers.

Chapter 5: The Thyme Has Come

The first fall frost signals the end of the gardening season, bringing with it a mixture of feelings—mostly regret that it's over, gratitude for a great harvest, and a little bit of relief. Each stored squash or bottle of fruit stands as a tribute to the efforts of the provident gardener. Practicing good harvesting and storage techniques can provide bountiful meals from the harvest long into the cold winter days when snow covers the garden and the fire burns brightly.

HARVESTING

Harvest time is the payday of gardening. One of the most important parts of gardening with edibles is to know exactly when the harvest time has come! Some things if picked prematurely will lack texture and flavor, or if harvested too late might be mushy, tough, and past the peak of flavor.

Different crops require different harvest tips. They can vary with the weather and the vegetable or fruit involved. For example, tomatoes can be left on the vine to fully ripen or they can be picked when partially ripened. On the other hand, crops like winter squash need to stay on the vine until fully developed and may even be at their best after a light frost.

Nothing tastes better in the spring than the first salad made from freshly-picked lettuce. These tender and delectable spring greens can be harvested much earlier than you might suspect. (See chapter 3 for cold frame ideas.) The outer leaves of lettuce and chard can be cut as soon as they are big enough to eat. You can leave the crown of the plant intact so new leaves will continue to grow. For spinach, harvest just the leaves at first, but then cut off the plant right at the soil line before it sends up a flower stalk.

STORAGE

Now that the produce is harvested, proper storage techniques mean the difference between fresh vegetables that can last for months and limp, squishy, unrecognizable lumps of rotting somethings.

Start with only the very best vegetables—you know what they say about one bad apple spoiling the whole barrel. Watch carefully for ripe produce. As vegetables continue growing and developing, they can quickly get past their prime and become overripe. The less fruits and vegetables are handled, the longer they will stay good when stored, so take care not to bruise them during harvesting. Typically when we think of the harvest, crisp autumn days and the crunch of leaves underfoot comes to mind. In a provident garden, the earlier and longer the harvest, the better!

Different vegetables require different conditions for storage. The main things to consider are temperature and humidity. Storage conditions can be divided into three categories:

- Cold and moist (32–40 degrees F and 95% relative humidity)
- Cold and dry (32–40 degrees F and 65% relative humidity)
- Cool and dry (50–60 degrees F and 60% relative humidity)

It's sometimes difficult to achieve optimal storage conditions at home. You may need to improvise and combine different methods to suit your situation. Even being able to store produce from the garden for a few weeks will seem like a taste of heaven compared with most store-bought fruit and vegetables.

Basements/Cold Storage Rooms

Basements are usually cool. If you have a source of water nearby or a high water table, keeping the optimum humidity levels may be easily done. In arid climates, basements are often dry as well as cool. One way to increase relative humidity is to occasionally give the basement floor a sprinkling of water, but only in the storage area. A cold-storage room can be created in a basement by partitioning off an area and adding some insulation. If there is a window in the room, the temperature can be controlled by opening or closing the window as needed. The stored crops should be well ventilated.

Refrigerator

Refrigerators are cool and dry. Because the cubic feet of space is limited and usually used for day-to-day produce—and humidity is lacking—the family's fridge is not usually a long-term storage option. However, an additional refrigerator in the garage or basement may be just the ticket for some extra storage. To create a cold and moist condition in the refrigerator, use perforated plastic bags. Sealed bags create condensation and aid in the growth of bacteria and mold. Even if you aren't aiming for long-term storage, you can fill up the refrigerator with as much produce as possible when you know a frost is in the forecast.

Root Cellars

If you are fortunate enough to have a root cellar, it provides an environment that is cold and moist for storage. A "mock" root cellar can be constructed out in the garden by burying a large barrel or container partially in the ground. Leave it at an angle for easy access. Then insulate the top with 12 inches of straw and soil over the backside of the barrel. Place boards that can easily be lifted off the straw layer in front to access the lid. The lid should be loose so air can circulate. Protect it so the barrel doesn't fill with rain or melting snow. A mixture of root crops can be placed inside and easily accessed. A simple "root cellar" can be made by burying a cooler in the ground and storing the root crops right there. Keep the lid slightly ajar to let in some air.

Sand

Root crops also store well layered with moist sand inside of a box or plastic container. Place the container in a cool, frost-free location, where it will remain for several months. (It's heavy when full). Add a layer of moist sand, then a layer of root crops. Continue alternating the layers until you finish with a layer of sand on top.

Ground

Some crops, such as carrots, can be stored right in the ground, covered with a thick layer of mulch and harvested later in the winter. If you have the room, a 12–18-inch deep trench can be dug. Make it as long as you need and then line the bottom and sides with burlap or woven weed barrier. Place the root crops in the trench and cover with sand or mulch. Cover the trench with plastic. When you want to harvest, shovel off the snow (if you are fortunate enough to have snow), peel back the plastic, and raid your larder.

Harvest and Fresh Storage Chart

CROP	WHEN TO HARVEST	HOW TO STORE
Beans	Pods snap easily; thinner than a pencil.	Cold and moist for short-term storage.
Beets	Beets are 1½–2 inches in diameter. Beet tops can be eaten as greens.	Store for up to 5 months in cold and moist conditions.
Broccoli	Cut buds before they begin to flower. Leave 5–6 inches of stem. Side shoots will then form and can be harvested.	Cold and moist for short-term storage.
Brussels Sprouts	Sprouts should be firm and about 1 inch in diameter. Start harvesting from the bottom up.	Store for 1 month in cold and moist conditions.
Cabbage	Cut heads when firm and solid but before they split open.	Store up to 5 months in a cold and moist environment.
Carrots	Harvest when ½–1 inch in diameter by loosening soil with a digging fork. Pull up needed carrots and trim off leaves.	Store in garden under a heavy mulch. Or store in a root cellar or container of moist sand. (See "Thyme to Dig In.")

Cauliflower	Cut heads when firm and compact.	Cold and moist up to 3 weeks.
Corn	Pick corn when the silk starts to turn brown. The kernels should be milky and plump. This is about 20 days after the silk first appears.	Cold and moist for 5 days.
Cucumbers	Harvest most cucumbers when they are 6–8 inches long for slicing, 4–6 inches to make dill pickles, and 2 inches long for baby dills. They should be crisp and dark green in color.	Refrigerate for up to 1 week.
Eggplant	Eggplant is ready to harvest when 6–8 inches long and a deep color. Pick when glossy and use a knife or scissors to cut from the plant.	Cool spot in house for about a week. Do not store for long periods under 50 degrees.
Lettuce	Outer leaves of lettuce can be cut as soon as they are big enough to eat. Always leave the crown of the plant intact so new leaves will continue to grow.	Cold and moist for 1 week.
Kohlrabi	Harvest when 3 inches in diameter.	Cold and moist for up to 2 months.
Onions	Harvest green onions when tops are 6 inches high. Harvest dry onions after green tops are ¾ dried. Loosen soil with a spading fork and gently lift out onions. Dry for a couple of days in the sun after digging. Brush off soil and dry for another 2–3 weeks. The papery skin layers should be crispy dry and the greens should be totally dry and tan in color. Some onions store better than others, so keep track of which variety you are growing.	Dry storage with good air circulation. Large onions seem to store better than small ones, so use those little ones first. Don't store near apples.

Peas	Harvest snow peas with edible pods when they are tender, flat, and bright green. Harvest English or Southern peas when they are young, tender, full, and round. When harvesting either type, use two hands to avoid uprooting the vine.	Cold and moist for up to 1 week.
Peppers	Harvest at any size. They will be sweeter the longer they are left on the plant. Hot peppers should be left on the plant to ripen to full color. Beware—the oils in hot peppers are transferred to your skin when you handle a cut pepper.	Refrigerate for up to 1 week.
Potatoes	Harvest new potatoes when the plant has finished blooming—leave plant intact to continue producing. Dig larger potatoes after vines die back. Use a spading fork to prevent cutting potatoes with a shovel. Lay potatoes on the soil to dry. Brush off soil before storing.	Store in a well-ventilated, cool, dry location for up to six months. See "Thyme to Dig In" for more info. Don't store near apples.
Radishes	Start thinning and eating radishes when they are a little larger than marbles. As they mature, they quickly become pithy and hot.	Cold and moist for 1 month.
Rhubarb	Harvest for 8–10 weeks after the third year. Don't harvest the first year and only 1–2 weeks the second year. Do not eat the leaves! Pull outer stalks rather than cutting. Leave at least one-third of the plant intact.	Cold and moist for up to 1 month.
Spinach	Harvest tender leaves of spinach. Cut right at the soil line before it sends up a flower stalk.	Cold and moist for 10–14 days.

Summer Squash	Enjoy while small—about 8 inches in length. Scallop squash are also best when small. They grow quickly, so check often. Remove and discard very large fruit.	Cold and moist for up to 1 week.
Swiss Chard	Cut outer leaves when 8–10 inches long. Leave crown of plant in place to continue growing.	Cold and moist for 1 week.
Tomatoes	Pick tomatoes when they are just yielding to the touch and have completely changed color. At the end of the season, pick fruit that has started to change color to ripen indoors. And don't forget to enjoy some fried green tomatoes.	Cool and dry. Do not refrigerate. Store in bowl at room temperature and daily rotate position of tomatoes. Ripen green tomatoes indoors between 60 and 72 degrees. Wrapping individually in newspaper will slow ripening. Tomatoes can be disinfected by wiping them with weak bleach solution and drying them thoroughly before storing.
Winter Squash	Harvest pumpkins and winter squash when the vines have died back but before a heavy frost. Leave 3–4 inches of stem intact. The skin should be colored and hard with a dull finish.	Cool and dry storage for 2–6 months. See "Thyme to Dig In."

Thyme to Dig In

Storing Carrots in the Ground over the Winter

Remove all weeds—no sense wintering over weeds.

Since the carrot tops will die down, mark where the roots are located.

Add a thick layer of straw or leaves as a mulch over the carrots so the ground will not freeze. The straw can be covered with something to hold it in place to keep it from blowing away and the leaves can be put in large garbage bags. This will make it easier to get to the carrots if there is snow on top.

Harvest the carrots as needed throughout the winter. In the early spring, harvest the remainder so that the carrots don't go to seed. (You can always leave a couple of carrots in the ground if you DO want them to go to seed.)

Thyme to Dig In

Potatoes

At the end of the growing season, the tops of the plants will turn yellow, then brown, and die down completely. An early frost will speed up this change. Carefully dig up the potato plants and sift through the soil to find all the potatoes you possibly can.

Once the potatoes have been dug, leave them on the soil for a little while to completely dry. Wet potato skin is very fragile, and if there is any damage to the skin, that potato will not store well. Burlap or paper bags make good storage containers if your harvest is a plentiful one. To keep for an extended period,

the potatoes must be kept cool. Potatoes kept in a refrigerator will convert some of the starch to sugar and will become sweet. You can remedy some of that sweetness by taking the potato out of the refrigerator a few hours before you plan to cook it.

Thyme to Dig In

Pumpkins and Other Winter Squash

Once the skin of the pumpkin hardens, the squash can be picked and eaten. Scratch the skin. If clear liquid immediately fills the scratch, the fruit is not ready. If the scratch remains dry, maturity has been reached. Toward the end of the season, removing the little green pumpkins and the blossoms will direct all the energy of the vine into ripening the earlier, larger squash.

Pumpkins must be mature and then cured (no, they don't have a disease) before being stored. The first light frost heralds the end of the growing season, and at that time the pumpkins are as mature as they will get. The best place to store pumpkins and other large winter squash—for the short run—is out in the pumpkin patch. This is true whether or not there has been a frost. But forecast of a hard freeze means you should pick the pumpkins and put them where they

won't be damaged. Leave at least 2 inches of the stem attached to the pumpkin when you harvest.

Ten days or so spent in the sun without freezing weather will start curing these future jack-o'-lanterns and sources of holiday pies. After that, a couple of weeks in a warm house will finish toughening the skin of the pumpkin. With stem intact and skin cured, it's time to lightly wipe down the pumpkin with alcohol or a weak bleach solution to remove any fungal spores. Dry completely, then lightly wipe with a little vegetable oil, and take them down to the basement to store. Don't place a winter squash on a concrete floor—moisture will condense and rot may start. If you have a back bedroom where the heat isn't used except when Grandma comes to visit, then place the pumpkins under that bed. It's a good place to store them.

Thyme to Dig In

Ethylene gas occurs naturally in nature and is the ripening agent that causes fruits to ripen and then decay. Apples particularly give off this gas, so when stored in close proximity to other vegetables and fruits, it will result in quicker decay. Store apples in their own location and keep them away from the rest of your harvest.

On the flipside, if you have something you WANT to ripen, such as pears, place an apple in a paper bag with the pears and the ethylene gas produced by the apple will ripen the pears.

CANNING AND DRYING AND FREEZING—OH, MY!

It seems that every neighborhood has one—the man or woman who effortlessly does it all. Not only do they and their family grow and produce a garden overflowing with abundance, but they also bottle . . . and can . . . and freeze . . . and dry all that produce until their storage room is overflowing.

If this were a musical, Reb Tevye would begin singing, "Tradition!" Gardening and preserving the results are superb traditions, but they must be adapted to personal circumstances and desires.

Preserving the Harvest

Storing fresh produce for as long as possible is the most nutritious option, but this method is short-term at best. Canning, freezing, and drying provide more long-term storage options, so pick the method that best suits your lifestyle and needs.

Karen's thoughts on such traditions stem from long-ago tender memories:

"On a late summer day many years ago, I watched with fascination as my great-grandmother sat in the backyard with a paring knife peeling apples as she prepared to make and bottle applesauce. I sat on the lawn in front of her waiting for the single, long, curling peel to fall into the pan on her lap. It was almost as good eating the tasty peel as it was the entire apple!

"Annually, generations before me filled mason jars with jewel-colored fruit and vegetables—pears, peaches, raspberries, dill pickles, dilly beans, beets, and pickle relish. My grandfather was in charge of the jam and made delicious peach/clove jam and my favorite—raspberry. The two best jars of each variety were carefully polished and set aside to be entered into the Morgan County Fair, usually to be adorned with a long blue ribbon.

"Onions were carefully dried, squash stored in the barn, French-cut beans salted in a crock, and apples picked—all for winter consumption. My grandmother felt that newly bottled produce was best left untouched until Thanksgiving, when the first taste of the year's dill pickles and beets then complemented the turkey dinner.

"For many years bottling homegrown produce was a standard I set for myself. It was a tradition after all—a late summer ritual that should be done—and if not done, then I felt self-imposed GUILT. Yep, that's right—guilt. As much as I think I would like to live in the simpler 'back when,' and follow in the footsteps of my grandparents, in my fast-paced world, it just isn't possible for me to preserve and bottle as much as I would like. At the same time, I want to not only store a bounteous harvest but also continue the tradition of generations and pass it on. Now, as a compromise, I bottle only our absolute favorites—and I've found freezing the harvest instead to be a quick method I can do on the run."

For Joy, the feel of autumn in the air brings to mind delicious thoughts:

"In September I find myself sniffing the air—yearning for the telltale aroma that assures that my family will have chili sauce for another year. During my elementary school days, I would smell Mom's chili sauce simmering blocks before I reached home. I knew what I would find when I went through the front door: Mom and Grandpa would be using a hand grinder to process the tomatoes, green peppers, and onions. Grandpa Percy always ground the onions because the fumes made Mom cry terribly. After the veggies were mixed in the large pot, in would go the sugar, vinegar, and spices. I think Mom always timed it so the first, or sometimes second, batch was on to simmer just as school let out. Even if it is only a half batch, I try to put up a few bottles of chili sauce each year just so I can close my eyes and see Mom and Grandpa working together in the kitchen."

Freezing

Freezing is hands down the easiest and quickest way to preserve fresh fruits and vegetables right out of the garden. Small batches can be done as the produce becomes ripe, and little equipment is needed—only space in your freezer and plastic bags or containers. Most vegetables that are usually cooked before eating can be easily frozen. Vegetables that are eaten raw such as lettuce, celery, or cucumbers shouldn't be frozen.

Vegetables to be frozen should be harvested first thing in the morning when they are at their freshest. When vegetables are picked, natural plant enzymes start to break down and result in loss of color, texture, and flavor. For this reason vegetables need to be blanched immediately after picking by either boiling or steaming them for a specified amount of time. This stops the conversion to starch process and leaves the vegetables tasting fresher. After blanching, the vegetables are immediately plunged into ice water

Thyme to Dig In

Joy's Grandma's Chili Sauce

4 green peppers, seeded
8 medium onions
24 medium tomatoes, peeled and cored
1½ tsp. cinnamon
1½ tsp. allspice
1 tsp. ground cloves
4 tsp. salt
1 pint sugar
1 pint white vinegar

Run peppers and onions through a hand food grinder (or chop in food processor).

Cut tomatoes in quarters; mix onions, peppers, and tomatoes in a large kettle. Add remaining ingredients. Bring to a boil and simmer 3–4 hours, until thick.

Fill hot canning jars in a hot water bath process for recommended time. Check with the extension office in your area for processing time.

to stop the cooking process. Once cooled and drained, the vegetables are packed into airtight bags or containers and frozen.

Nut trees make great additions to the edible landscape. After a few years, gardeners find the quantity of nuts each year outpace the family's ability to eat them. Freezing is a great way to preserve these lovely sources of protein and healthy oils. Shell the nuts, keeping kernels as nearly whole as possible. Spread in a thin layer to dry for 24 hours. Package the nuts in airtight bags for freezing. Nuts keep well frozen up to 6 months. Salted or seasoned nuts do not keep nearly as long.

Fruit does not require the blanching process. Many fruits, especially berries, freeze very well.

After washing and drying small fruit, put them on a cookie sheet and freeze before putting them in a freezer bag or container. You can pour out just a few or enough for a pie recipe without thawing the entire batch.

Drying

Drying vegetables for later consumption is the oldest method of preservation. This is an inexpensive and very convenient way to store. Drying requires some sort of heat to remove the moisture from the

Thyme to Dig In

Blanching cleanses the surface of dirt and organisms, brightens the color, and helps retard the loss of vitamins. Blanching also wilts or softens vegetables and makes them easier to pack.

Use a wire blanching basket and covered saucepan, or fit a wire basket into a large kettle with fitted lid. Use 1 gallon of water per pound of prepared vegetable. Put vegetables in blanching basket and lower them into vigorously boiling water. Place lid on blancher and start counting blanching time as soon as the water returns to a boil. (The water should return to boiling within 1 minute, or you are using too much vegetable for the amount of water). Keep heat high for total blanching time.

Blanching time is crucial and varies with the vegetables and size. Under-blanching stimulates the activity of enzymes and is worse than no blanching. Overblanching causes loss of color, flavor, vitamins, and minerals.

"How to Blanch," National Center for Home Food Preservation.

Blanching times for some veggies:

Snap beans	3 minutes
Broccoli	3 minutes (boiling water)
Carrots	1 minutes (diced, sliced)
Cauliflower	3 minutes (florets, 1 in)
Onion rings	10–15 seconds
Peas, edible pod	1½–3 minutes
Peas, green	1½ minutes

produce to prevent spoilage. Drying time varies from vegetable to vegetable and from fruit to fruit.

Drying can take place in an oven, in a commercial countertop dehydrator, or even in the sun under the right conditions.

Canning

When done correctly, canning is a safe method for preserving food. Basically, fruits or vegetables are placed in jars and heated enough to destroy microorganisms that cause food to spoil. As the jar cools, a vacuum seal is formed and a satisfying "click" signals it is sealed—music to the canner's ears!

More equipment is needed for canning than for freezing or drying, but after the initial investment, only replacement lids need to be purchased.

Food is processed either in a boiling water bath (tomatoes, fruits, pickles, jams, or jellies) or in a pressure canner (vegetables and meats). Once processed, food can last for up to two years on the shelf.

COUNTY EXTENSION OFFICES

Whether one or a combination of preserving methods is used, proper and safe techniques need to be utilized. The best source of this information is at local county extension offices. They always have the most up-to-date instructions for all methods and can provide tips and hints on preserving food safely. Take the time to visit your local extension office to discover a wealth of information or even to take a class or two.

Thyme to Dig In

The moisture content of home-dried fruit should be about 20 percent. When the fruit is taken from the dehydrator, the remaining moisture may not be distributed equally among the pieces because of their size or their location in the dehydrator. Conditioning is the process used to equalize the moisture. It reduces the risk of mold growth.

To condition the fruit, take the dried fruit that has cooled and pack it loosely in plastic or glass jars. Seal the containers and let them stand for 7 to 10 days. The excess moisture in some pieces will be absorbed by the drier pieces. Shake the jars daily to separate the pieces and check the moisture condensation. If condensation develops in the jar, return the fruit to the dehydrator for more drying.

Vegetables should be dried until they are brittle or "crisp." Some vegetables actually shatter if hit with a hammer. At this stage, they should contain about 10 percent moisture. Because they are so dry, they do not need conditioning like fruits.

So Easy to Preserve, 5th ed., 2006. Bulletin 989, Cooperative Extension Service, The University of Georgia, Athens. Revised by Elizabeth L. Andress. PhD, and Judy A. Harrison, PhD, Extension Foods Specialists.

Gaining some experience in all methods of preservation allows a gardener to have food stored and ready to eat, whatever circumstances are at hand. As with all phases of gardening, practice will make for confident and successful processing and storage. A provident gardener with an edible landscape and storage skills will have food from his or her own garden to enjoy every day of the year.

FAQs

How do you save sunflower seeds?

Mammoth Sunflowers are the variety usually grown if you plan on saving seeds. Because birds will be way ahead of you noticing when the seeds are nearly ripe, you'll need to protect the flower heads from them. When the seeds barely begin to change from greenish to a darker color, wrap the entire flower in a brown paper bag and secure the bag with string. The covering must allow good air circulation so mold won't ruin the seeds. Check weekly until you can easily shake or rub the seeds from the flower head. Or cut the flower from the stalk and take indoors to finish maturing and drying. The heads should be bent over and the back of the flower turning yellow before you cut the flower. You can get over one thousand seeds from a large sunflower!

How do you roast pumpkin seeds?

Here is one way, compliments of www.simplyrecipes.com.

Toasted Pumpkin Seeds

One medium-sized pumpkin
Salt
Olive oil

Preheat oven to 400°F. Cut open the pumpkin and use a strong metal spoon to scoop out the insides. Separate the seeds from the stringy core. Rinse the seeds.

In a small saucepan, add the seeds to water—about 2 cups of water to every ½ cup of seeds. Add a ½ tablespoon of salt for every cup of water (more if you like your seeds saltier). Bring to a boil. Let simmer for 10 minutes. Remove from heat and drain.

Spread a tablespoon of olive oil over the bottom of a roasting pan. Spread the seeds out over the roasting pan, all in one layer. Bake on the top rack until the seeds begin to brown, 10–20 minutes. When browned to your satisfaction, remove from the oven and let the pan cool on a rack. Cool the seeds before eating.

How do you freeze tomatoes?

Rather than bottling or drying tomatoes, you can freeze them. One way is to core and peel each tomato. Put them on a cookie sheet in a single layer and freeze overnight. The next day you can put them into gallon freezer bags to store for months. When thawed, tomatoes lose their firmness but retain their fresh flavor for use in soups and sauces.

How do you dry apples?

Nothing tastes better in the winter than dried apples sprinkled with a little cinnamon and sugar. A great and not very expensive investment is a combination corer, peeler, and slicer and a countertop dehydrator. Slice the apples to a thickness of ⅜-inch, treat with lemon juice to prevent browning, and place in a dehydrator for 6–12 hours until pliable. If desired, sprinkle lightly with cinnamon or sugar before drying. Store in a jar and enjoy!

What do you do with a huge banana squash?

A full-size banana squash is usually more than one family can eat after cutting. Cut pieces can be stored in the refrigerator for a few days. Bake any excess cut pieces until they can be mashed with a fork. Remove the rind, puree in a blender, and pour into a plastic bag in serving-size portions, then freeze. Delicious for months to come!

How do you freeze fresh herbs?

Herbs with a high water content often mold before they are dried, so freezing is a great alternative. Pick healthy leaves, wash, and pat dry with a paper towel. Freeze individual leaves on a tray, then store in the freezer in a closed container. When done this way, the leaves won't freeze together and can be used as needed. Another method would be to wash, pat dry, and chop into small pieces. These can be stored in individual serving-size plastic bags or placed in an ice cube tray with a little water, frozen, and then stored in plastic bags to use in cooking.

CONCLUSION:
Ready, Set, Grow

We believe the time is approaching when the opportunity to choose to be a provident gardener will have come and gone. Either we will have put into practice the idea of cultivating an edible landscape or we will regret that we didn't. The chapters in this book were designed to encourage you to look beyond perceived limits. You determine what you can do to grow your own food. You *can* make a difference in the way you become prepared for the future.

You and your extended family and friends can decide how well the adventures coming up will stretch your ingenuity. Fear is a terrible place to start your decision-making and planning. Talking about possibilities stirs anxiety. Planting encourages confidence. Projecting the difficulties dampens thoughts of solutions. Stacking bottled peaches and pickled beets stimulates satisfaction. Calling out dangers, calamities, and emergencies creates feelings of doom. Learning new methods of cultivation expands the feeling of hope and faith.

Many notable people have understood that what you think determines what you can accomplish. Or as Helen Keller put it, "Optimism is the faith that leads to achievement. Nothing can be done without hope and confidence."

Buoy up your confidence—you *can* create a productive garden. Enjoy the one little cherry tomato that ripened just before the frost. Know that next year in the garden you will do even better.

Start small—seed by seed, plant by plant, and space by space. Sow the seed that is the love of gardening in the hearts of your children and grandchildren.

Scatter those seeds among your neighbors. Share the knowledge of seed planting with everyone you meet. The harvests will long outlive your lifetime, maybe even the lives of those children you teach. What an incredible legacy!

Gardens aren't necessarily planted to make or save money. Most gardeners realize this fact somewhere along the line. It can be really disheartening to try and make the bottom line justify all the effort. As Andy Rooney once said, "Last night, we had three small zucchini for dinner that were grown within fifty feet of our back door. I estimate they cost somewhere in the neighborhood of $371.49 each."

The first few times planting a garden, as we've said before, can take more than it gives. But each successive garden will multiply the bounty. Good tools line the wall of shed or garage, soil becomes rich and nourishing, preserving methods start to seem like second nature, and pleasure radiates in wider and wider circles around you. Even little containers produce more after the first few seasons.

Once you establish a rhythm, your garden becomes worth way more than you initially spent. Instead of trying to calculate the monetary value of the seeds you sow, the hours spent cultivating, and the store price of sixteen quarts of bottled tomatoes, look higher for the value of your gardening. This is the ultimate exercise in faith, hope, and obedience. We believe, as Christian Nestell Bovee wrote,

"To cultivate a garden is to walk with God."

Decide this day to join us in this most wonderful walk. Come along—and along the way create your own incredible, edible landscape.

Happy and provident growing!

Joy & Karen

APPENDIX

ZONES

On most plant tags, in tiny print, there is a designation showing in which zone the plant will grow, which is all fine and good except where do you find *what* zone you're living in and, more important, what *is* a zone?

At some point in every gardener's life, they will fall in love with some plant just because they love the plant! Maybe it is the creamy white of the gardenia blossom; maybe it's the impressive huge flowers of a Saucer magnolia; or it certainly could be the heavenly fragrance and fruit of an orange tree. Some get taken by the lovely spring flowers of a lilac or the fruit and fall color of a blueberry bush or the gorgeous fanlike leaves of a palm tree.

When you are so smitten, you start looking around to find who is already growing your newfound love. Hmmmm—nary a one to be seen. Now, how can that

PLANT HARDINESS ZONE MAP

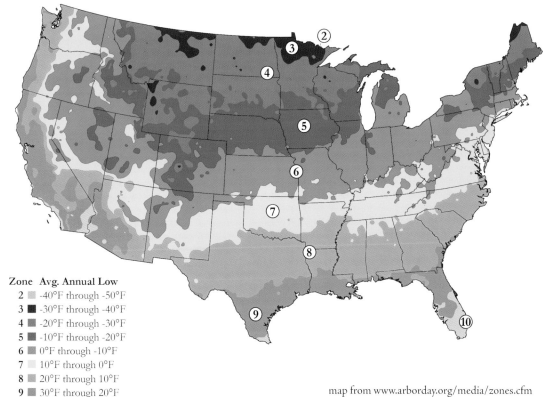

Zone	Avg. Annual Low
2	-40°F through -50°F
3	-30°F through -40°F
4	-20°F through -30°F
5	-10°F through -20°F
6	0°F through -10°F
7	10°F through 0°F
8	20°F through 10°F
9	30°F through 20°F
10	40°F through 30°F

map from www.arborday.org/media/zones.cfm

be? How can gardeners on your street, in your town, or in your city be unaware of how spectacular this plant would be in their garden? So you head to your local nursery or garden center to solve the mystery of the unplanted beauty.

If you chance upon a gentle soul with years of gardening experience, they will smile kindly and explain, "In this zone, we can't grow that plant." A younger, less restrained employee may burst out with an embarrassing, "You want to grow *that* HERE? You're kidding, right?" Both have the information you wanted, or rather, didn't want to know. Because of elevation or summer heat or winter cold or the wrong soil or lack (or excess) of humidity or length of growing season—or a nasty combination of two or more of the above conditions—it is futile to try growing your beloved plant.

The Department of Agriculture puts together a map of the various regions of the United States with divided and color-coded areas that have approximately the same low temperatures during the winter. Plant zones range from 1 (plants that will tolerate temperatures of minus 50°F) to 11 (plants that will only tolerate temperatures 40°F and above). Other organizations like ArborDay.org put together similar maps. Calculated to help gardeners keep from freezing the knees off of plants that couldn't live in temperatures that dipped below, oh say 40 degrees, the zone tolerance was then printed on plant tags. Mighty fine idea! Except for a few hitches that developed in this "git along":

- These zones only consider winter cold temperatures with nothing said about blistering summer heat.
- There is no mention of tolerance for high or low humidity.

- The need for a specific soil alkalinity or acidity isn't mentioned.
- The tags never explain if Zone 4 is warmer than Zone 6—it is assumed that everyone who buys a plant with a tag already knows this.
- If a plant is listed as Zone 4 (pretty cold weather) in the northeast part of the country, will it still grow in Zone 7? Will it make it through a winter or summer way down in the southern states?

Then to add to the confusion—there are other designations of zones chosen by other garden entities that don't match up at all with the USDA map and zones. And there is still another zone map designed to indicate how hot the summers get in a given area. Some plant tags say in small print that "this is a perennial" but in even tinier print it's listed as Zone 9. Well, partner, Zone 9 never sees so much as a frost, let alone a single snowflake. One winter in an intermountain garden, and that little perennial shows itself to be a very expensive annual!

Here is an example of a zone designation, sort of. Sort of because there are exceptions and differences of opinions:

Salt Lake City, Utah, is Zone 5-ish. Most Zone 4 plants do well and more and more varieties that are listed as Zone 6 grow well here, thank you very much. Rarely can we stretch to safely grow plants from Zone 7, but that doesn't keep some of us from trying!

In my fifty years of paying attention to plants and especially their flowers, I can tell you that the growing season here has lengthened and moderated. Plants that could be counted on to provide flowers for Memorial Day now blossom nearly two weeks earlier, leaving little to pick for bouquets to decorate the graves. This shift in season has also increased the number of plants we can now plant with increasing confidence that they will make it through our winter.

To determine what zone your garden is in, you can consult a map or, better still, contact a local Master Gardener or extension office. They can give you a zone number and also the exceptions and cautions.

PLANTING CHART

One of the most frequently asked questions is when to plant what. A lot of variables are involved in that answer, but hopefully this chart will simplify some of that. Don't forget—the weather can change this time schedule from year to year, so these are "abouts."

TYPE	PLANTS	PLANTING TIME	COMMENTS
Hardy Plants	Asparagus, Broccoli, Cabbage, Onions, Peas, Spinach, Radish, Rhubarb	Mid-March in Zone 5	Plant as soon as you can work the soil. This goes for Zones 3 and 4 as well.
Half-Hardy Plants	All of the above, plus: Beets, Carrots, Cauliflower, Lettuce, Potatoes, Swiss Chard	Toward the end of March in Zone 5	Depends on if the snow has melted in Zones 3 and 4.
Tender Plants	Beans, Corn, Cucumbers, Summer Squash	Mid- to end of May	Or about when apple blossoms first appear. Zones 3 and 4 need to be prepared with protection from frosts.
Very Tender Plants	Cantaloupe, Peppers, Winter Squash, Tomatoes, other melons	End of May to first part of June	Plant when the soil is warm. Again, cover up if in a colder zone.

FROST MAP

The last frost date for an area is the last day in the spring that it's likely you'll have a frost. It's important to recognize that the actual date of the last frost is different every year. It can be much earlier than the average or much later. This is especially important to note because tender plants can be killed in one night by a frost. For hardier plants, the average last frost date is more of an indicator of general growing conditions than a danger sign.

Microclimates play an important role in frost dates. Features like hills or water can significantly affect temperatures. There could possibly be a different actual last frost date just a few houses away.

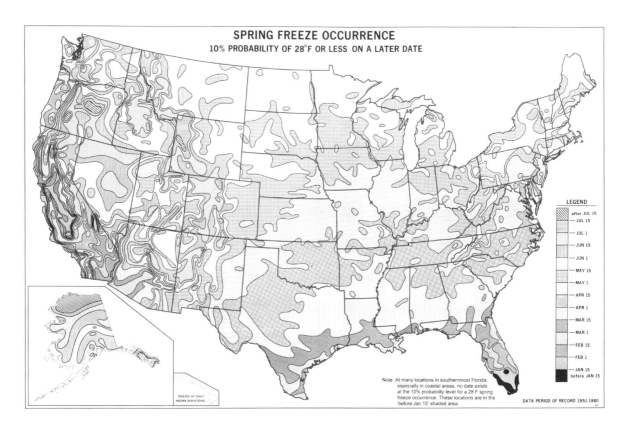

Map from the NOAA Satellite and Information Service, http://www.ncdc.noaa.gov/oa/climate/freezefrost/frostfreemaps.html.

ORGANIC ANIMAL CONTROL

Natural Remedies to Keep Critters Away

REMEDY	PROBLEMS	REMEDY	PROBLEMS
Cayenne pepper, sprinkled on vegetable leaves (spray first with water)	Keep away rabbits	Fences	It's always a good idea to keep large animals from the garden, but it takes an eight-foot fence to keep out deer.
Plastic utensils	Keeps cats away. Yes, really! Stick plastic forks, knives, or spoons in an area that has been newly planted with seed. This will keep cats from using it as a litter box until the seeds sprout and the plants grow.	Protective cages	Individual cages made from chicken wire can be placed over garden boxes or sections of a garden to protect from animals.
Rotten egg, garlic mixture, spoiled fish (or any combination of the above)	Deer don't like really bad smells. A mixture like this will keep deer away—may also work on unwanted visitors as well.	Scarecrows, Mylar streamers, wind chimes	A combination of these scare off birds for a short time. Move and change the display regularly so that the birds don't get used to it.
Soap from hotels	Deer are repelled by the smell of *strong* soap. Hang soap from trees, or nail to stakes or fence posts.	Flour and cayenne pepper (1 cup flour to 2 table-spoons cayenne)	Sprinkle on cabbage to keep out the cabbage worm. The flour gets the cabbage worm and the cayenne pepper takes care of other pests.
Human or animal hair	Deer stay away from the smell of human or animal hair—the longer and more unwashed the better. Sprinkle it around the garden or hang in little mesh bags about three feet off the ground. Must be refreshed about once a month, more often if it rains or snows.	Neem oil— Commercial (2 tablespoons per gallon of water. Mix frequently as you spray. Completely wet tops and undersides of leaves.)	Many uses—insecticide, miticide and fungicide. Controls various diseases as well as insects and mites. Use on vegetables, fruit trees, and ornamentals.
Wire mesh	To keep burrowing animals from popping up in your garden and if you are using garden boxes, attach fine wire mesh to the bottom of the boxes before filling with soil. Keeps kitties from using garden areas as a litter box when laid flat on the ground and covered with a very light layer of mulch		

BISCUITUS DELICIOSA

Family: Pastriaceae (pay-stree-ay'-see-ee)

Genus: Biscuitus (bis'-kit-us)

Species: deliciosa (dee-lis-ee-oh'-suh)

[Do not mistakenly plant the less desirable B. vulgaris "Chips Ahoy."]

NOTE: *By carefully taking into account photoperiod, nighttime temperatures, and late spring frosts, gardeners should be able to manipulate ripening date to coincide with any child's birthday.*

Although the species and varieties of Biscuitus are nearly endless, the most endearing and evocative is *deliciosa*. So easily hybridized that almost everyone's grandmother grew subspecies or even developed a new variety, the fruit is still universally recognized. Whether it's the old standby "Chocolate Chip" or the supermarket "Chips Ahoy," Americans love their Biscuitus deliciosa!

Biscuitus fruit can be found in great variety at most retail centers. The varieties purchased, however, can never match the flavor, aroma, and texture of the ones home grown. Our British counterparts usually refer to these tasty fruits by their generic name—Biscuits. In America we prefer the common name—Cookies. As with all common names, this can lead to confusion between species and varieties, but nearly everyone recognizes B. deliciosa as "Chocolate Chip."

Biscuitus species cross very easily, and hybridizing can become a passion for gardeners at all levels of expertise. A favorite parent species is B. scottii, or "Scottish Shortbread." This simple, unassuming little plant can become quite spectacular when crossed with B. arachis, B. ribes, or B. avena. These crosses result in such well known varieties as: Raisin Cookie, Oatmeal Cookie, and Peanut Butter Cookie. Further crosses have given rise to the exquisite "Chocolate Chip Oatmeal Raisin" variety. These have led to the many numerous regional varietal favorites.

The common characteristics of the shrubs are similar for all varieties and cultivars. They naturally form a moderately dense, dark green bush that is 4–5 feet tall and 3–4 feet wide. Occasionally a branch will revert back to a parent strain, B. scottii usually, and these sports should be pruned out immediately.

In the intermountain region, plant the seedlings on the north or east side of a home, fence, or other structure. Begin with a careful selection of the best seed. Choose only the freshest and smallest seed available. The larger seeds often result in a malady found in the ripening fruit known as "crumble."

The ripening fruit can tolerate, at most, two to four hours of direct sunlight. Too much direct sun and the fruit buds will drop prematurely and ruin the entire harvest. This loss of fruit is a condition commonly known as "early season meltdown."

TOWERS OF POTATOES

No room in your garden for rows of potatoes? Grow them vertically in a potato tower! Not only can you expect a large harvest for a small space, but you also don't have to weed the potato patch!

Towers can be constructed using a variety of materials. A circular wire cage, barrel, or wooden box can be constructed and used—even a stack of old tires if appearance isn't an issue. Any bottomless container that can hold mulch or loose soil will work. The tower should be about 24–30 inches in height and approximately 20 x 20 inches at the bottom.

No matter the tower used, plant 3–4 nice healthy seed potatoes in the bottom of the tower. Cover with 4 inches of soil. As the vines grow, keep adding more soil or mulch, covering all but one-third of the plant's new growth. Repeat until the tower is full. Don't forget to water consistently—the soil in a tower can dry out quickly. Yukon golds and other early varieties of potatoes don't do as well in towers because they set fruit all at once and so only produce in the first 6 inches. Varieties to try in a tower would be Yellow Finn, Binjte, Red Pontiac, or the fingerling types.

A wooden tower can be built with four 2 x 2 supports screwed on the inside of four 2 x 6 boards. As the potatoes grow, four more 2 x 6 boards are added. This process is repeated until the tower is at the top of the 2 x 2's. To harvest new potatoes, simply unscrew the bottom 2 x 6's, reach into the loose soil, and twist off the desired potatoes, leaving the plant intact. Replace the 2 x 6's, and the next time you want new potatoes, go to the next level. When it's time to harvest the potatoes, unscrew all the boards and unearth your treasure.

**A UNIQUE POTATO TOWER
MADE FROM OLD TIRES**

ALL THE
BEST
COMPOST

What Is Compost?

Sometimes referred to as "black gold for the garden," compost is a rich supply of organic nutrients in the form of dark, mostly decomposed, organic matter. There is nothing better to add to garden soil year after year than this wonderful substance.

Think about walking through a forest breathing in the moist earthy fragrance that pervades the air. The ground is soft and spongy underfoot, and the trees, bushes, and wildflowers grow with wild abandon. It is an experience to be savored. This is brought about in part by nature's compost covering the forest floor.

To a lesser extent, the same conditions can be re-created in your own yard and garden. Taking a deep breath of homemade compost can suddenly transport you back to the forest. Sometimes we think that bottled eau de compost could be the perfume of choice for true gardeners!

Where Does Compost Originate?

The never-ending cycle of birth, life, and death creates the sources of natural compost. Some years, some centuries, some eons are more conducive to compost formation than others. Climate patterns shift and so does the time frame for the decomposition that leads to compost. Fires destroy large swaths of forest and leaf mold grinds to a halt for years and years. A flood ravages along a great river and between the silt and the dying plant material, compost is formed quickly, allowing for a rich harvest within a year. Man-made, or man-gathered, compost is more regimented in its origin.

Commercial bags or bulk piles of compost are created from specific sources, depending on which company is making and marketing the compost. A mushroom growing enterprise sells the spent mushroom compost. Those who raise turkeys combine turkey droppings with wood shavings, compost it for a given length of time, and bag turkey compost. An egg-raising company found a use for the other end product of their chickens and so bag chicken compost. Some companies send individuals for training to perfect their composting process and then earn a much sought-after certification as Certified Organic Compost for their product. The Organic Materials Research Institute (OMRI) and the Rodale Institute certifications are a couple of the trusted names in organic certification. The "certified" part concerns the sources of organic material, not just the actual end product, since by definition all compost is organic.

Where Can You Get Compost?

While much of the compost sold is in bags of one size or another, it is also possible to get compost in bulk. The nurseries, garden centers, and landfills that sell in bulk usually require you to show up with a trailer or truck, and they load the compost for you. Other companies will deliver either bag or bulk compost, usually for the cost of the product plus a delivery fee. For an exotic source of compost, check out the nearest zoo. Some animal parks collect and compost their animal waste and, after composting it, sell to the public.

It is usually best to stay away from compost from waste-treatment plants. We've heard stories about people who have used it, and added water, and it somewhat reconstituted into . . . well, you get the picture. Better safe than sorry!

A new company is doing a double duty of keeping tons of waste from the local landfill and creating rich compost at the same time. This group of energetic enterprising young men formed a company that connects with supermarkets and local restaurants to collect food that would ordinarily be sent directly to the "dump." Through a proprietary process they create rich, dark compost. From their website they explain: "A cubic foot bag of our finished product reduces greenhouse gasses as much as parking your car for one month! Instead of clogging landfills and gassing the air we breathe, EcoScraps products enrich your soil, helping you grow healthier plants in the most environmentally friendly way."

What Should You Compost?

You can do basically the same thing in your own garden. Collect all vegetable scraps plus shredded paper to take outside to compost. There are attractive "compost buckets" that can be kept on the counter until you're ready for a jaunt to the great outdoors. Stainless steel, porcelain, colored plastic, faux wood—buckets to fit any decor. To speed the composting process to the max, run the veggie pieces through the blender before sloshing them into the bucket. Eggshells can be added to the blender mix. Eggshells left whole will be intact for ages—or at least several years.

Some people go so far as to have a vermiculture composting system in their kitchen. In other words, that's a bin full of red worms who continually work on composting the kitchen scraps added. You have to ask yourself if you really *want* a container of worms in your kitchen, but it does produce a nutritious compost to add to the garden.

Paper that has been shredded will break down quite quickly in the composting process. Newspaper can be added by the single sheet, but if you shred or tear it into strips, it will decompose faster.

The following is an overview of ideal compost materials gathered from the great outdoors:

Grass clippings (if no weed killer was used on the lawn, and none of the weeds in the lawn have started going to seed) are a good addition to the compost. Because clippings are mostly water, they tend to pack down and can make a slimy mess. Layer them with other material. Grass clippings can also be dried first and added later.

Leaves, dry or fresh, are usually easy to find. Try to avoid using leaves from any plants that show symptoms of diseases.

Small sticks and branches will help allow air circulate in the pile.

Leftover produce from the garden, especially at the end of the season, works well. If any seeds were

already mature, you may get volunteer plants popping up around the edges of your compost pile. Pumpkin seeds seem especially able to take advantage of the rich warm soil at the bottom of the compost.

Weeds that haven't gone to flower or seed can be disposed of in the compost. Don't use them if they were sprayed with a weed killer. If a compost pile heats up properly, the temperature is high enough to render seeds unviable, but don't risk this. Eliminate as much weed seed as possible from the compost.

Old straw that may have been used as mulch will continue to break down in a compost pile.

Sawdust or wood shavings add carbon and allow for air circulation. When great quantities of this raw organic matter are used, there may be a need to add extra nitrogen to keep the microorganisms growing during the composting process. This can be done by layering the wood product with fresh grass clippings or by adding a nitrogen-rich fertilizer. Should you be blessed with chickens, the chicken manure would be perfect.

Rabbit pellets—that is, rabbit droppings—are a near perfect addition to the compost pile. They add needed nitrogen and break down very quickly. The rabbit pellets used as food for the bunnies are also high in nitrogen, usually from alfalfa, and can be added to the compost pile as a nitrogen booster.

Manure can be added as long as it isn't from a meat-eating animal. Fresh manure needs to be well-composted so it isn't too "hot" for the plants.

ABCs and 123s of Composting

Making your own compost doesn't need to be complicated—in fact, it can be a very simple process. For years, after hearing a lecture on composting, Karen decided it was much too complicated of an ordeal to even attempt. Instructions were given to dig a deep

Thyme to Dig In

Five Ingredients for Great Compost:

- Brown stuff—leaves, dry grass clippings, shredded branches
- Green stuff—fresh grass clippings, veggie trimmings, fresh plants
- Dirt—a trowel full or two
- Water—enough to make the "stuff" good and damp
- Air—good air circulation is vital

If your leaves are big and you want to cut them up a bit, spread them over the driveway and run over them with the lawn mower. With the bag on, you can collect the bitty leaf pieces easily.

Layer about a third of a black plastic bag with leaves, then green stuff, and then dirt. Then layer again and add a bit of nitrogen fertilizer to speed things up. Place it someplace where it can stay over winter and poke holes in the bottom of the bag. Sprinkle with lots of water to get the contents all damp. Leave the top open. The top leaves don't change much, but the ones further down in the bag compost nicely.

trench, add a lot of organic material, send away for a box of red worms (small snakes in Karen's opinion), spread the worms over the organic matter (you mean, touch them?), fill the trench in with soil, wait a long period of time, dig up the trench again, and there should be your finished compost. Whew! Makes you exhausted even reading about it.

All those steps are totally unnecessary. Here is a much simpler process:

- Prepare a structure to hold the material. This can be a series of wooden pallets fastened together forming bins, a more formal and nice-looking wooden bin, or a commercial composter. However, using no structure at all is fine; just pile the stuff on the ground.

- Add ingredients—use a wide variety of material (see p. 110 for ideas). The smaller the pieces, the quicker you get finished compost. Layer the material, thinking in opposites: green, then brown; wet, then dry; coarse, then fine . . . you get the picture. Add some rich soil or compost every couple of layers as a starter for the pile.

- The size of the pile should be at least 3 feet by 3 feet and no bigger than 5 feet by 5 feet so there is enough bulk to heat up in the center, but not so big it can't be turned.

- Add enough water to the pile so that it is evenly moist without being sopping wet.

- Turn the pile regularly with a pitchfork to allow air to circulate and to allow all ingredients a chance to be in the middle where the fastest, hottest decomposition takes place. Turning weekly would be ideal. Every few weeks would be fine.

- Compost is finished when it is a rich, dark, good-smelling earthy material and there are no identifiable ingredients. That said, some material takes longer to break down and so a sieve can be used to screen out coarse material in order to begin using finished compost. The coarse material that is screened out goes right back into the unfinished compost pile to continue decomposing.

You may like to use a very simplified trench method. This works quite well if you have only a little kitchen waste at a time to add to the composting process. Along one edge of the garden, or garden box, dig a 6-inch deep, 6- inch wide trench, or a 6 x 6-inch hole. (Don't fret the measurements—it's just a little hole.) As a section of the trench fills, cover with the soil you piled next to it. Keep filling and covering and then extend the length of the trench or dig more little holes as the season goes along. The following year, start your trench on the far side of your garden bed. The previous season's underground compost should be ready to be mixed with the surrounding soil and planted as usual.

The question is always asked how long it takes for compost to be ready for use. The answer depends on climate conditions and the effort spent. In hot, humid climates, the finished compost can be ready in just a couple of months. In the dry mountain west, it can take up to a year. Chopping ingredients into small pieces, keeping the pile moist, and moving (or turning) it at least weekly can speed up the process. On the other hand, the ingredients can be piled together and left alone, and compost will form in a couple of years (think the forest floor).

Lights, Camera, Action

So, exactly what happens in that compost pile to turn scraps and waste into black gold? As fungi and bacteria begin to break down the organic matter, heat is created. The smaller pieces of the pile begin to lose form. Soon it is hard to recognize the lettuce and other small or soft pieces of the original pile. As the breakdown continues, heat waves may be seen to rise from the pile. Even in the winter, an active compost pile will steam. Temperatures inside the pile are often around 140 degrees or higher when tested with a long compost thermometer. Mold and other fungi can be seen on the surface of the remaining large pieces, like maybe a chunk of orange peel. Later, the bottom of the pile will start to take on the characteristic brown, crumbly nature of compost even as the edges and top are continuing to break down.

As the compost nears completion, the inner and lower sections of the pile are nearly all crumbly-brown and earthy-smelling. Only the woodiest portions of the original pile can still be recognized as what they were in the beginning. Soon the compost is in the form that most gardeners would pay good money for. Nutrients in this rich, homemade compost are readily absorbed by green plants. These plants live, then die, and are added to a compost pile. The process is now complete, and ta-da! We're back where we started, with a new pile of raw organic matter. Time marches on.

It is very productive to have several compost bins in various stages of decomposing if you have the space. A series of three bins works well—one bin full of the organic material, an empty bin next to it to use when turning the pile back and forth, and one bin with finished, ready-to-use compost.

To Add or Not to Add, That Is the Question

The Adds

Add anything that was once living to the compost pile. The list is endless and as you start to look around your home, you'll be amazed at the number of ingredients just waiting to be recycled into dark, rich compost. Here's a sampling of the "adds":

- Grass clippings (dry first)
- Leaves
- Weeds, without flowers or seeds. Grassy weeds should not have roots attached.
- Newspaper (shredded is best)
- Wood chips
- Sawdust
- Shriveled apples, peaches, pears, apricots, and on and on
- Fruit rinds
- Garden plants (without signs of disease)
- Shredded paper (finally—a use for junk mail)
- Old lettuce, carrots, and so on from the fridge
- Coffee grounds
- Tea bags
- Shredded branches
- Small twigs
- Peelings from apples and potatoes
- Aquarium water
- Used potting soil
- Foliage from spring bulbs
- Flowers
- Crushed egg shells
- Corn husks (cobs take a long time to compost)
- Wood ash (in limited amounts)
- Cardboard
- Dryer lint (from natural fibers)
- Hair (yes, that's right)

The Add Nots

Although barnyard animals and rabbits and llamas produce jim-dandy manure that can be composted for use in the garden, cat and dog droppings should never be used in compost headed for the garden. Disease organisms that can be transferred to people can be found in those droppings. Even fresh cow or horse manure can cause problems in the compost if the pile isn't run as a "hot" pile. When temperatures reach 140 to 160 degrees, weed seeds are effectively killed. These weed seeds come compliments of whatever weeds the horses or cows have been eating lately. Compost that isn't heated to that degree will be a terrible source of new weeds in your garden.

Kitchen residue often contains baked, dairy, or meat products. Don't add these to the compost pile. They tend to rot and will attract flies and other undesirable pests like mice and rats. To sum it up, don't add:

- Manure from meat-eating animals
- Baked goods
- Dairy products
- Meat products
- Field bindweed, commonly known as "morning glory" (Yes, it could go in the compost pile, but why risk it? This not-so-glorious weed is like a cat—it has at least nine lives!)

Black Gold Is Wealth Untold

Compost in large quantities should be incorporated in all beds before planting, after planting, after harvesting, at the beginning of the growing season, at the end of the season, and any time in between any of the above! When you make your own black gold, you usually get relatively small amounts at a time, and this is most effective if you mix it with the soil going back into individual planting holes.

Adding compost to a garden can be achieved in several ways—purchased or homemade. For either type, these basic principles apply:

- Mix and use a variety of types of compost—the more the better. Even though eating a tomato is healthy, if that were the only food ingested, it wouldn't be a balanced diet. The same is true of compost. Using compost made from just one ingredient doesn't offer the variety of nutrients needed for healthy plant growth. In a homemade compost pile, add many, many different ingredients. If purchasing bags of compost, read the label and make sure it contains at least five or six different components, or buy several bags of different types and mix them together.

- Compost must be decomposed properly. Poorly composted manure is too "hot" for plants, usually from too much nitrogen. Often, purchased bags of composted manure are rushed too soon to market without having completed the decomposing process. If you open a bag and the smell is more like the barnyard than the forest, then that is a good indication it needs more time to process. The simple solution is to put it aside and use that bag next spring or work it into the soil in the fall and let it sit over the winter. Most green waste compost that is done incorrectly will smell of ammonia and sulfur or will get soggy and really stink from anaerobic bacteria.

- Dark, rich compost makes a great top-dressing or mulch for the garden and can be worked in later to help condition the soil. When put down as a top dressing of one or two inches in a planting bed, compost will create a mild compost tea as moisture percolates through it. This moisture can come as natural precipitation or additional watering by a gardener. The roots of plants can easily absorb the nutrients from this "liquid compost," and beneficial microorganisms in the soil are improved as well.

Green Reasons to Make Black Gold

Individuals and households contribute a horrendous amount of compostable waste to local landfills every day. You can reduce your negative impact on landfills, and the environment in general, by putting your green waste to work in your own garden. If you are currently bereft of a garden, we can only hope the area where you live is making available a "green waste" receptacle so you can send your appropriate kitchen waste to a location that creates compost. If you enjoy your garden but don't currently compost your own materials, be sure to send all the green products you can to the community composting location.

The end result for making your own compost will be bigger, healthier plants and tastier, more nutritious produce. What more could a gardener ask?

GARDEN STORAGE

Food storage is a topic that has been written about in dozens and dozens of books. It has been spoken of over pulpits and on news broadcasts. Most people are at least familiar with the idea of having extra food on hand and usually include other staples like toilet paper, soap, Band-Aids, and shampoo. Others aim to store a few weeks worth of everything their family uses. But have you thought of storage for your gardening needs?

Storing Knowledge

Having a helpful reference base to rely on is important. Books and periodicals stay functional even if the electricity is off. Why should electricity matter? It does matter if the only place you go for your information is the Internet. Even the most seasoned and experienced gardener occasionally needs to be reminded when to prune a raspberry cane or whether to fertilize strawberry plants before or after they produce the berries. Printed sources are also a great place to learn about things never before attempted.

Though basic information is critical, it is fun to have ideas about new ways to try growing old favorites. There are books about growing just tomatoes and books that are nearly encyclopedic on growing every vegetable and fruit you might like to try. Start with a general A to Z guide like the *Sunset Western Garden Book*. Then add a specialized book, like one on pruning. Starting from seed can be a real challenge, but a book with helps and hints will boost your confidence.

It is advisable to have general guides for construction in the garden as well as growing in the garden. Novice gardeners can make grow boxes, plant supports, and cold frames if they have some first-rate instructions. Gardeners also need access to some basic building tools: a hammer, a screwdriver, pliers, wrenches, a good measuring tape, a level, a variety of nails and screws, wood glue, and duct tape. Some garden supplies and implements you can't build for yourself, so it's a fine idea to have some extras stored; there may be times you can't just run to the garden center to buy a replacement.

Tooling Around

Sturdy, well-built tools can last for decades. Spending a little extra the first time around will save you money and aggravation in the future. Shovels and rakes with one-piece construction of the metal parts can take a lot of wear and tear. Always choose the kind that has rivets holding the handle to the metal or the wonderful construction grade types that are one solid piece from top to bottom. Try to avoid the kind that has the wooden handle jammed into the end piece.

Even with an investment in excellent equipment, things can break or wear out. A couple of spare long, wooden handles can double or triple the life of the working end of a shovel or hoe. Extra care at the end of the gardening season will extend the usefulness of those wooden handles. Go over the wood with fine-grade sandpaper and then apply a light coat of boiled linseed oil to preserve the wood. The metal end of

tools should be cleaned with soap and water and then given a light coat of oil. A bucket with sand and a few ounces of used motor oil will clean and protect the metal heads of shovels, hoes, and rakes. Just jab the head of each tool up and down in the oily sand. The abrasive sand, together with the tiny metal filings from the used oil, finishes the cleaning job, and the oil prevents any rust from forming over the winter. A good file will allow you to keep the edge of your shovel, spade, and hoe nice and sharp. Trowels can be the two-dollar variety, bending

the first time you apply pressure, or they can be the ten-dollar cast aluminum style that will be passed on to your grandchildren. While you're out buying a top-notch trowel, buy one as a spare. No gardener ever regretted having too many trowels. Purchasing a durable pair of hand pruners is another case of extra dollars well spent.

Some types of hand pruners can be disassembled and the worn parts replaced. Be sure to buy the replacement parts at the same time you buy the pruners. Sharp pruners, whether loppers or hand pruners, make any job easier. Buy a sharpener that is recommended for the type of blade on the tool or purchase a multipurpose sharpener that can handle several blade types. You will be surprised at how much easier it is to do your gardening with a sharp tool versus one that is dinged up and dull.

To save your back and make garden work quicker, buy a high quality garden cart or wheelbarrow. Whether it has pneumatic tires or those made from solid plastic, buy two or three extra tires for storage. If your cart has wooden handles, treat the wood the same as you do your shovel handle.

The Supporting Cast

Out in the garden, you will find many plants that need a little extra boost to stay upright, so plan on buying or building good plant supports. Plant supports should be placed when the plants are still small, so have these on hand before the plants start to fall over. When buying cages for tomatoes, don't underestimate the value of paying a little more to get the tallest, sturdiest ones available. Take good care of these supports, and you'll have years of tomato success. You can also make your own tomato supports using something like concrete reinforcing wire. Remember to buy a pair of heavy-duty wire cutters if you're tackling this project. Wire cutters will also come in handy when constructing things out of chicken wire, like tree trunk protection.

Bundle Up

In areas where late spring frosts and early fall freezing temperatures may cut short your gardening season, stockpile protection for your garden plants. It won't cost much to have a few packages of Frost Blanket or some other kind of lightweight covering for the garden. You can make your own little individual plant protectors out of plastic milk bottles. Cut the bottom off gallon milk bottles and then nest them one inside another and hang them up in the back of your storage area. They won't take up much space, and it will be easy to put them in place at a moment's notice.

Having a few old sleeping bags or quilts on hand to throw over the garden on frosty nights can save a crop. Because of the sleeping bags' weight, a few dowels pounded into the ground can protect the plants from being crushed. Lightweight plastic over the whole thing can keep it dry and cozy.

Chemical Warfare

As much as we dislike chemical warfare in the garden, certain products do have their advantages. Glyphosate (one well-known brand name is Round-Up) is a high-quality, non-selective herbicide. It kills everything green it hits. Well, not exactly everything. Mostly, it's success is inversely proportional to how much you want the plant killed. But it is still a useful product to have on hand. Keep it from freezing, and don't store it in a shed that gets very, very warm. Glyphosate will stay good for years. You can buy a smaller container, and get the same amount of useful product, if you buy the highest concentration of active ingredient. Always store any herbicide or pesticide in the original container.

Another product to consider for your garden storage program is slug and snail bait containing iron phosphate. A current brand name is Sluggo. There is also a combination of iron phosphate and a botanical insecticide that will help control earwigs—Sluggo-Plus is an example of this kind of product. These kinds of bait are safe to use around kids, cats, dogs, and other favored critters.

Seeds, Seeds, Seeds

Chapter 3 talks about seeds and the advantages of open-pollinated and hybrid varieties of vegetables. Learning to gather and store open-pollinated seeds is a very useful piece of knowledge. But buying and correctly storing hybrid varieties is also a handy

thing to do. Small bottles like pint canning jars can be used to store several packets of the same hybrid variety of seeds. Buy your favorite varieties and pack them, along with a small amount of anti-desiccant in the jar, label the bottle, and top with a canning ring and lid. If stored in a cool, dark place (like a cellar or basement cool room), most seeds will last for years and years. Buy these packets when you find them because you never know when they will disappear from the shelves—not just because they were sold out, but maybe because the seeds weren't available to be packaged.

Along with the seeds, you will need little containers in which to start your seedlings. These can be purchased or improvised. Some items worth saving for seed starting are empty yogurt containers, egg cartons, and clear plastic produce boxes. (The produce boxes can be lined with paper towels and turned into little teeny greenhouses.)

You will need some sort of growing medium for these containers. A really good product will be labeled specifically as seed starting mix and is usually a combination of peat moss and vermiculite. Vermiculite, which is puffed mica rock, is particularly suited for storage since it doesn't matter if it dries out. Premium potting soil will work to start seeds, but if the bag is stored for a long time and allowed to dry out, it is nearly impossible to get it to retain moisture again.

Making a List and Checking It Twice

Post the following list, or one that fits your circumstance, and start checking off the storage items as you get what you need for your garden. Provident gardening goes hand in hand with an edible landscape: both begin with thinking ahead to things that might come. Plus, it is comforting to know you will have just what you need, when you need it. Whether it is having a good hand trowel for planting your young tomato plants or fetching a couple of bottles of green beans for dinner, planning ahead will assure you will have both whenever you need them.

This suggested storage is a very general list. But you need to start somewhere, so circle a few items and go from there. Individualize the list with other things that come to mind.

Provident Gardening Storage List

- Basic gardening information; how-to and when-to books*
  - *Joy in Your Garden*
  - *Burpee Seed Starter: a Growing Guide*
  - *The Pruning Book*
  - *Western Garden Book of Edibles*
  - *Sunset Edible Garden*
  - *The Edible Garden*
    * all found in our bibliography
- Bottling supplies
  - Pressure canner for non-fruit, non-acidic produce, and meat
  - Boiling water canner
  - Canning bottles (not old salad dressing jars)
  - Rings and lids
  - Pectin for jam and jelly (fairly short shelf life—just a few years)
- Building tools
  - Wire cutters
  - Pliers
  - Wrenches
  - Hammer
  - And so on

- Chicken wire
- Dehydrator
  - Cheesecloth (use outdoors to keep insects from fruit)
  - Screen (for homemade version)
- Duct tape
- Fertilizer (slow release, organic if possible)
  - As long as it is kept dry, fertilizer is good for years. The exception: mycorrhizae (beneficial microorganisms) stay viable for only a year or so. Seaweed extract is a mild organic fertilizer for seedlings and other young plants.
- Frost blanket
  - Row cover/reemay
    - Both are for frost protection, a deer deterrent, and an insect barrier
  - Garden staples
    - These hold down the lightweight garden cover (easier to use than boards or rocks)
- Gardening tools
  - Extra long handle for shovel
  - Hand tools like trowels and hand pruners
  - Sharpeners for all types of blades on mowers, pruners, and so forth
  - Sandpaper
  - Boiled linseed oil
  - Sand with used motor oil
- Gloves
  - You can't have too many. Most wear out within a season. Ones with cuffs help keep the dirt out of the gloves.

- Lawn bags
  - Plastic garbage type or compostable paper ones
- Plant supports
  - They can be fashioned out of nearly anything. Many commercial kinds are decorative as well as functional (support for pole beans, peas, tomatoes, young trees)
- Seeds
  - Some of your favorite hybrid varieties (see chapter 3)
- Envelopes to save seeds
- Containers to store seeds
- Vermiculite
- Snail bait
  - Sluggo/Sluggo Plus
- Twine
- Water hose, extra
  - Hose ends/menders
  - Gaskets for sprinklers/hoses
- Weed killer
  - Concentrated Round-Up

BIBLIOGRAPHY

1. Adams, Abby. *The Gardener's Gripe Book: Musings, Advice and Comfort for Anyone Who Has Ever Suffered the Loss of a Petunia.* New York: Workman Publishing, 1995.

2. Ball, Jeff. *Jeff Ball's 60-Minute Garden.* Emmaus, PA: Rodale Press, 1985.

3. Boland, Maureen, and Bridget Boland. *Old Wives' Lore for Gardeners.* New York: Farrar, Straus and Giroux, 1976.

4. Bossi, Joy, and Karen Bastow. *Joy in Your Garden.* Springville, UT: Cedar Fort, 2010.

5. Bremness, Lesley. *The Complete Book of Herbs: A Practical Guide to Growing & Using Herbs.* New York: Viking Studio Books, 1988.

6. Buckingham, Alan, and Jo Whittingham. *Grow Vegetables.* New York: DK, 2008.

7. Coulter, Lynn. *Gardening with Heirloom Seeds: Tried-and-True Flowers, Fruits, & Vegetables for a New Generation.* Chapel Hill: University of North Carolina Press, 2006.

8. Crockett, James Underwood. *Crockett's Victory Garden.* Boston: Little, Brown and Company, 1977.

9. Emery, Carla, and Lorene Edwards Forkner. *Growing Your Own Vegetables: An Encyclopedia of Country Living Guide.* Seattle: Sasquatch Books, 2009.

10. Fell, Derek. *Vegetables: How to Select, Grow and Enjoy.* New York: HP Books, 1982.

11. Freeman, Criswell, ed. *The Gardener's Guide to Life: Timeless Lessons Based on the Principles of Gardening.* Nashville, TN: Walnut Grove Press, 1997.

12. Green, Donna. *Days to Remember: A Keepsake Book for Birthdays, Anniversaries & Special Occasions.* New York: Smithmark Publishers, 1995.

13. Hamilton, Geoff. *Organic Gardening.* new ed. New York: DK, 2011.

14. Heffernan, Maureen. *Burpee Seed Starter: A Growing Guide for Starting Flower, Vegetable, and Herb Seeds Indoors and Outdoors.* New York: Macmillan, 1997.

15. Hughes, Holly, ed. *Gardens: Quotations on the Perennial Pleasures of Soil, Seed, and Sun.* Philadelphia: Running Press, 1994.

16. Ishizuka, Kathy. *The Quotable Gardener.* New York: McGraw-Hill, 2001.

17. Lively, Ruth, ed. *Taunton's Complete Guide to Growing Vegetables & Herbs.* Newtown, CT: Taunton Press, 2011.

18. Lovejoy, Sharon. *Trowel & Error: Over 700 Shortcuts, Tips & Remedies for the Gardener.* New York: Workman Publishing, 2003.

19. Mittleider, Jacob R. *Mittleider Grow-box Gardens.* Salt Lake City, UT: International Food Production Methods, 1975.

20. Reich, Lee. *The Pruning Book.* Newtown, CT: Taunton Press, 2010.

21. Smith, Charles W. G. *The Big Book of Gardening Secrets.* North Adams, MA: Storey Publishing, 1998.

22. Smith, Edward C. *The Vegetable Gardener's Bible.* North Adams, MA: Storey Books, 2000.

23. Smittle, Delilah, and Sheri Ann Richerson. *The Complete Idiot's Guide to Year-Round Gardening.* New York: Alpha, 2010.

24. Staub, Jack. *75 Exciting Vegetables for Your Garden.* Salt Lake City, UT: Gibbs Smith, 2005.

25. ———. *75 Remarkable Fruits for Your Garden.* Salt Lake City, UT: Gibbs Smith, 2007.

26. Ward, John, ed. *The Backyard Builder: Over 150 Build-It-Yourself Projects for Your Garden, Home, and Yard.* New York: Wings Books, 1994.

27. *Western Garden Book of Edibles: The Complete A to Z Guide to Growing Your Own Vegetables, Herbs, and Fruits.* Menlo Park: Sunset, 2010.

28. White, Hazel et al. *The Edible Garden.* Menlo Park, CA: Sunset, 2005.

REFERENCES

BOOKS

All New Square Foot Gardening
Mel Bartholomew
Cool Springs Press, 2005

PERIODICALS

Country Gardens
1716 Locust St.
Des Moines, IA 50309-3023
www.BHG.com/countrygardens

Countryside & Small Stock Journal
145 Industrial Drive
Medford, WI 54451
Phone: (800) 551-5691
www.countrysidemag.com

Fine Gardening
63 South Main Street,
PO Box 5506
Newtown, CT 06470-5506
Phone: (800) 477-8727
www.finegardening.com

The Herb Companion
1503 SW 42nd St.
Topeka, KS 66609-1265
Phone: (800) 456-5835
www.herbcompanion.com

The Old Farmer's Almanac
PO Box 4002037
Des Moines, IA 50340-2037
Phone: (800) 256-2622
www.almanac.com/store

Organic Gardening
33 East Minor St.
Emmaus, PA 18098
Phone: (610) 967-5171
www.organicgardening.com

Zone 4
P.O. Box 3208
Bozeman, MT 59772
Phone: (406) 586-8540
www.zone4magazine.com

WEBSITES

Central Utah Gardens
www.centralutahgardens.org

Colorado State Extension
www.ext.colostate.edu

Conservation Garden Park
www.conservationgardenpark.org

Joy's Website
www.joyinthegarden.com

Ogden Nature Center
www.ogdennaturecenter.org

Red Butte Garden & Arboretum
www.redbuttegarden.org

Salt Lake County Extension
www.extension.usu.edu/saltlake

Thanksgiving Point Gardens
www.thanksgivingpoint.com

Utah County Extension
www.extension.usu.edu/utah

Utah Rose Society
www.utah-rose.com

Utah Water Garden Club
www.pondutah.com

Wasatch Community Gardens
www.wasatchgardens.org

Weber County Extension
www.extension.usu.edu/weber

Wheeler Historic Farm
www.wheelerfarm.com

Young Living Farms
www.youngliving.com/en_US
/company/farms/

And for fun, Jerry Goodspeed's:
"Do You Have a Gnome Problem"
at www.utahpests.usu.edu/htm
/factsheets/publication=8057
(click on "Download Now!")

CATALOGS

**Brown's Omaha Plant
Farms, Inc.**
110 McLean Ave. PO BOX 787
Omaha, TX 75571
Phone: (903) 884-2421
Fax: (903) 884-2423
Email: mail@bopf.com
Website: www.bopf.com

Family-owned business, 4 generations.
12 varieties of onions, 4 varieties of
sweet potatoes

Burpee Gardens
300 Park Avenue
Warminster, PA 18974
Phone: (800) 888-1447
Email: custserv@burpee.com
Website: www.burpee.com
Catalog request via regular mail:
032763 Burpee Building
Warminster, PA 18974

Flower and vegetable seeds and plants, some shrubs, vines, roses, hedges. Many hybrids. Some supplies.

The Cook's Garden
PO Box C5030
Warminster, PA 18974-0574
Phone: (800) 457-9703
Email:
cooksgarden@earthlink.net
Website: www.cooksgarden.com

Untreated seeds, many unique vegetables. Catalog interspersed with fun recipes. Many herb plants and seeds. 21 varieties of sunflowers.

Garden Burgess Seed & Plant
905 Four Seasons Road
Bloomington, IL 61701
Phone: (309) 662-7761
E-mail: customercare@
eburgess.com
Website: www.eBurgess.com

Usual flowers, shrubs, trees, veggies, and fruit. A few supplies.

Gardener's Supply Company
128 Intervale Rd.
Burlington, VT 05401
Phone: (888) 833-1412
Fax: (800) 551-6712
Website: www.gardeners.com

From super shovels to tractor scoots, plant shears, raised boxes, 4 sizes of bamboo stakes, gloves, and nearly anything you could use in a garden.

Gardens Alive!
5100 Schenley Place
Lawrenceburg, IN 47025
Phone: (513) 354-1483
Email: service@gardensalive.com
Website: www.gardensalive.com

Organic and environmentally friendly everything! Fertilizers, pesticides (including Escar-go), bird food, garden tools, and decorations.

Gurney's Seed and Nursery Co.
PO Box 4178
Greendale, IN 47025-4178
Phone: (513) 354-1492
Fax: (513) 354-1493
E-mail: service@gurneys.com
Website: gurneys.com

Fruit, vegetable, and flower seeds, fruit and nut trees, small fruit plants, and shrubs.

Henry Field's Seed and Nursery Co.
PO Box 397
Aurora, IN 47001-0397
Phone: (513) 354-1495
Fax: (513) 354-1496
E-mail: service@henryfields.com
Website: henryfields.com

Fruits, vegetables (especially onions), worms, organic pest controls, flowering trees, fruit trees, and small fruits.

Hartmann's Plant Company
PO Box 100
Larota, MI 49063-0100
Phone: (269) 253-4281
Fax: (269) 253-4457
E-mail: info@hartmannsplant
company.com
Website: www.hartmannsplant
company.com

Blueberries, strawberries, hardy figs, and Lingonberries!

Heronswood
300 Park Avenue
Warminster, PA 18974-4818
Phone: (877) 674-4714
Fax: (866) 578-7948
E-mail: info@heronswood.com
Website: www.heronswood.com

"Unusually Great Plants"—that's what the catalog says, and they are correct! Unusual perennials, shrubs, grasses, trees, ferns, or vines.

High Country Gardens
2902 Rufina Street
Santa Fe NM 87507-2929
Phone: (800) 925-9837
Fax: (800) 925-0097
Website: www.highcountry
gardens.com

Water-wise plants, perennials, cacti, succulents, shrubs, grasses, and herbs.

Honeycreek Nurseries
Division of Burgess Seed
905 Four Seasons Road
Bloomington, IL 61701
Phone: (309) 663-7359

Email: customercare@
honeycreeknurseries.com
Website:
www.honeycreeknurseries.com

Mostly perennials, shrubs, trees, groundcovers, bulbs, roses, and grasses

Jung

335 S. High St.
Randolph, WI 53956
Phone: (800) 297-3123
Fax: (800) 692-5864
Website: www.jungseed.com

100 years of seed growing! Large selection of flowers, nice selection of veggie seeds, and wide selection of supplies.

John Scheepers Kitchen Garden Seeds

23 Tulip Drive
PO BOX 638
Bantam, CT 06750
Phone: (860) 567-6086
Fax: (860) 567-5323
E-mail: Customerservice@
kitchengardenseeds.com
Website: www.kitchengardenseeds
.com

This is their 100th year! The usual plus some interesting unusual seeds for herbs and veggies. Several collections of seeds grouped together.

Miller Nurseries

5060 County Rd. NE
Canandaigua, NY 14424-8904
Phone: (800) 836-9630
E-mail: info@millernurseries.com
Website: www.millernurseries.com

Dwarf cherry trees, small fruits, hop vines, fruit trees, David Austin roses, elderberries, and figs.

Nichols Garden Nursery

1190 Old Salem Rd. NE
Albany, OR 97321
Phone: (800) 422-3985
Fax: (800) 231-5306
E-mail: customersupport@
nicholsgardennursery.com
Website:
www.nicholsgardennursery.com

Core sponsor of safe seed initiative (against genetically engineered plants or seeds), herb and rare seeds, herb plants, vegetable seeds, edible flower seeds, herb teas, essential oils, books, and recipes.

Oikos Tree Crops

PO Box 19425
Kalamazoo, MI 40019-0425
Phone: (269) 624-6233
Fax: (269) 624-4019
E-mail: customerservice@
oikostreecrops.com
Website: www.oikostreecrops
.com/store/home.asp

Unusual tree, shrub, and ground crop plants including 3 varieties of Jerusalem Artichokes! Wildlife forage crops of all kinds.

Park Seed

1 Parkton Ave
Greenwood, SC 29647
Phone: (800) 845-3369
Fax: (864) 941-4506
E-mail: info@parkscs.com
Website: www.parkseed.com

Huge range of perennials, vegetables, and herbs. Excellent roses. Helpful tools and supplies.

Peaceful Valley Farm & Garden Supply

POBox 2209
125 Clydesdale Court
Grass Valley, CA 95945
Phone: (888) 784-1722
E-mail: helpdesk@groworganic
.com
Website: www.GrowOrganic.com

Incredible selection of seeds, books, tools, sprinkler parts, helpful charts, organic nutrients, and more.

Pinetree Garden Seeds

PO BOX 300
New Gloucester, ME 04260
Phone: (207) 926-3400
Fax: (207) 926-3886
Email: pinetree@superseeds.com
Website: www.superseeds.com

Many open-pollinated varieties, French veggies, Italian veggies, continental oriental veggies, Latin American veggies, herbs, and rare plants.

Raintree Nursery

391 Butts Road
Morton, WA 98356
Phone: (800) 391-8892
Fax: same number
Email: customerservice@
raintreenursery.com
Website: www.raintreenursery
.com

Fruit trees, berries, vines, and unusual edible plants. From dwarf bananas and pomegranates to ginkgoes and licorice, you will find unique mouthwatering treasures.

Renee's Garden

6060A Graham Hill Rd.
Felton, CA 95018
Phone: (888) 880-7228
E-mail: customerservice@renees-garden.com
Website: www.reneesgarden.com

Flower, vegetable, and herb seeds. Unusual varieties from all around the world.

RH Shumway's Seedsman

334 W. Stroud St.
Randolph, WI 53956
Phone: (800) 342-9461
Website: www.rhshumway.com

Vegetable seeds, Jerusalem Artichokes, sugar beets, wholesale quantities, farm and field seed, and orchard grass.

Richters Herbs

357 Hwy 47
Goodwood, ON LOC 1A0
Canada
Phone: (800) 668-4372 or (905) 640-6677
Fax: (905) 640-6641
E-mail: orderdesk@richters.com
Website: www.richters.com

More herbs than you can shake a trowel at! 48 varieties of basil, and 35 varieties of mint.

Seeds of Change

PO Box 4908
Rancho Dominguez, CA 90220
Phone: (888) 762-7333
Fax: (320) 796-6036
Website: www.seedsofchange.com

The original keeper of heirloom seeds; all-certified, organic veggies, herbs, flowers, and an excellent selection of garden tools and supplies.

Seeds of Distinction

PO Box 86
Station A (Etobicoke)
Toronto, Ontario Canada M9C 4V2
Phone: (416) 255-3060
Fax: (888) 327-9193
Email: seeds@seedsofdistinction.com
Website: www.seedsofdistinction.com/news/news.htm

Many unique annuals, biennials, perennials, and bulbs.

Seymour's Selected Seeds

334 W. Stroud St.
Randolph, WI 53956
Phone: (800) 353-9516
Website: www.seymourseedusa.com

Familiar flower seeds, many unusual and English flower varieties, and a few vegetables including courgette!

Stark Bro's

PO Box 1800
Louisiana, MO 63353
Phone: (800) 325-4180
Fax: (573) 754-8880
E-mail: info@starkbros.com
Website: www.starkbros.com

Many original hybrid fruit trees, small fruits, ornamental trees, as well as familiar varieties.

Territorial Seed Company

PO Box 158
Cottage Grove, OR 97424
Phone: (800) 626-0866
Fax: (888) 657-3131
E-mail: info@territorialseed.com
Website: www.territorialseed.com

Vegetable, flower, and herb seeds; edible and ornamental plants; and garden supplies and accessories. They test and try every variety before putting them on the market.

Thompson & Morgan

PO Box 397
Aurora, IN 47001-0397
Phone: (800) 274-7333
Fax: (888) 466-4769
E-mail: service@tmseeds.com
Website: www.tmseeds.com

Assorted annual and perennial flower seeds, new and unusual vegetables along with a wide variety of typical favorites, and a great index.

Totally Tomatoes

334 W. Stroud St.
Randolph, WI 53956
Phone: (800) 345-5977
Website: www.totallytomato.com

Novelty tomatoes, new varieties, many heirloom varieties, and some peppers and cucumbers.

Van Bourgondien

PO Box 2000
Virginia Beach, VA 23450-2000

Phone: (800) 622-9959
Fax: (800) 327-4268
Email: blooms@dutchbulbs.com
Website: www.dutchbulbs.com

Selling in the US since 1893. Catalog has beautiful pictures. The spring catalog features gorgeous perennials, and the fall catalog has a huge selection of bulbs.

Vermont Bean Seed Company

334 W. Stroud St.
Randolph, WI 53956
Phone: (800) 349-1071
E-mail: info@vermontbean.com
Website: www.vermontbean.com

Untreated seeds, seeds from around the world (mostly veggies—lots of beans), some unusual flowers, and herbs.

Vesey's Seeds Ltd.

PO Box 9000
Calais, ME 04619-6102,
Phone: (800) 363-7333
Fax: (800) 686-0329 (24 hrs/ 7 days)
Email: customerservice@ veseys.com
Website: www.veseys.com

Short season specialties, vegetable, annual, and perennial seeds, garden tools and supplies, and organic pest control.

Wayside Gardens

1 Garden Lane
Hodges, SC 29695-0001
Phone: (800) 213-0379

Fax: (800) 817-1124
Email: info@waysidecs.com
Website: www.waysidegardens.com

Perennial plants, old roses, shrubs of all kinds, evergreens, hostas.

Willhite Seed Inc.

PO Box 23
Poolville, TX 76487-0023
Phone: (817) 599-8656 (local) or (800) 828-1840 (toll-free)
Fax: (817) 599-5843
Email: info@willhiteseed.com
Website: www.willhiteseed.com

Vegetable seeds, onion plants, French vegetables, Indian subcontinent vegetables, and more kinds of watermelon than you can shake a stick at.

INDEX
[Names of plants in italics]